UNTIL THEY ARE HOME

NUMBER 133:
Williams-Ford
Texas A&M University
Military History Series

UNTIL THEY ARE HOME

Bringing Back the MIAs
from Vietnam,
a Personal Memoir

Thomas T. Smith

Texas A&M University Press
College Station

First edition

This paper meets the requirements of ANSI/NISO Z39.48-1992 (Permanence of Paper).
Binding materials have been chosen for durability.

Library of Congress Cataloging-in-Publication Data

Smith, Thomas T., 1950–
Until they are home : bringing back the MIAs from Vietnam, a personal memoir / Thomas T. Smith. — 1st ed.
p. cm. — (Williams-Ford Texas A&M University military history series ; no. 133)
Includes index.
ISBN-13: 978-1-60344-232-9 (cloth : alk. paper)
ISBN-10: 1-60344-232-4 (cloth : alk. paper)
ISBN-13: 978-1-60344-233-6 (e-book)
ISBN-10: 1-60344-233-2 (e-book)
1. Vietnam War, 1961–1975—Missing in action—United States. 2. Smith, Thomas T., 1950– —Career in the Army. 3. Smith, Thomas T., 1950– —Travel—Vietnam. 4. Joint POW/MIA Accounting Command (U.S.) 5. United States—Foreign relations—Vietnam. 6. Vietnam—Foreign relations—United States. 7. Vietnam—Description and travel. I. Title. II. Series: Williams-Ford Texas A&M University military history series ; no. 133.
DS559.8.M5S64 2011
959.704'38—dc22
[B]

2010022442

Dedicated to the remarkable young military men and women and their civilian teammates who work with unwavering heart and unfailing commitment in dark and dangerous places to find answers for the families of the lost ones

Our mission continues . . .
Until They Are Home!

—Joint POW/MIA
Accounting Command

[W]hat is so appealing about Asia, the chance to journey through a dream . . . and abandon yourself to other forces; . . . Anything is possible. Vietnam revealed itself to me as a land of parallel universes . . .

—Carsten Jensen,
I Have Seen the World Begin: Travels through China, Cambodia, and Vietnam

CONTENTS

Introduction 1

1. To the Far Shore 6

2. Taphonomics 10

3. *La Rue Sans Joie* 22

4. My Hometown: Hanoi 35

5. Politics 47

6. Crossing the River Styx 62

7. Vientiane and Phnom Penh 73

8. Chasing Odysseus 80

9. Christmas and Tet 95

10. "That Is Sooooo Vietnam" 104

11. *Ông, Văn Phòng* MIA–*Hoa Kỳ* 111

12. The Last Flight 121

Afterword: November 2009 127

Index 129

UNTIL THEY ARE HOME

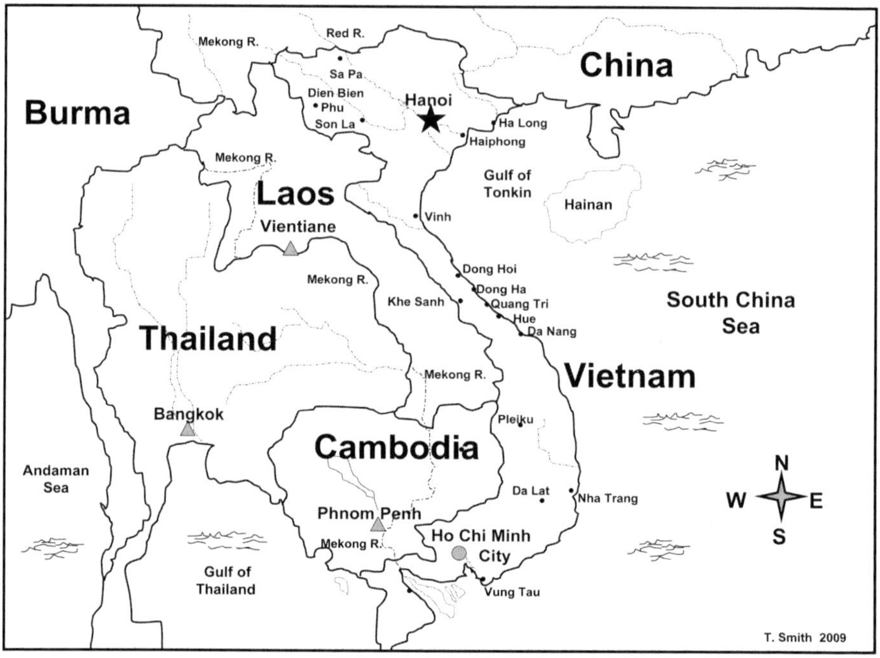
Mekong R.
Red R.
China
Sa Pa
Dien Bien
Phu
Hanoi
Burma
Son La
Ha Long
Haiphong
Mekong R.
Gulf of
Tonkin
Laos
Hainan
Vinh
Vientiane
Dong Hoi
Mekong R.
Dong Ha
Khe Sanh
Quang Tri
South China
Sea
Hue
Thailand
Da Nang
Vietnam
Mekong R.
Bangkok
Pleiku
Cambodia
Andaman
Sea
N
W
E
S
Da Lat
Nha Trang
Phnom Penh
Ho Chi Minh
City
Mekong R.
Gulf of
Thailand
Vung Tau
T. Smith 2009

INTRODUCTION

I WAS A FIFTY-TWO-YEAR-OLD U.S. Army lieutenant colonel returning to Viet nam thirty-one years after I had been there as a kid in the U.S. Navy during the war. I was beginning to feel ancient and a bit beat up but put on my uniform and boots every day with a grin, lucky to love my duty, unlike so many civilian friends I knew who were trudging uphill into their fifties carrying the heavy rucksack of professional slump, dreading sunrise and each day of a work that had lost its light.

Although much of my career was spent in a standard track, assigned to infantry battalions, I also had a pattern of doing and enjoying odd jobs for the government. I taught military history at West Point, went to graduate school in history at Texas A&M University, had a secondary specialty as an army historian, and published five books. For three years I ran counterdrug operations on the Mexican border and then became the garrison commander, sort of a city manager, for the U.S. Army War College at Carlisle Barracks, Pennsylvania, before becoming a war college student.

When I started my student year, I began considering my next assignment, which might be at the Pentagon, which I had avoided in the past and in fact had visited only once in my entire career, or I would more likely be given an unaccompanied overseas assignment—without family—to one of the "forgotten Stans"—Uzbekistan, Kyrgyzstan, Tajikistan, and so on, which seem to be the fate of many war college graduates lately. Facing a one-year tour without my wife and seeing my children, I decided to try to do something personally meaningful. I wanted to go to Vietnam and command the MIA search teams. I had been paying attention to reports on this mission for several years as a succession of friends had the fortune to earn this duty and command the detachment in Hanoi.

In 1985, when I was a captain attending the Infantry Officer Advance Course at Fort Benning, Georgia, we shared a beautiful old two-story duplex with Capt. Mike Peppers and his family. After Mike became a lieutenant colonel and had successfully commanded a battalion, a prerequisite for the assignment, he was selected to go to Hanoi in 1999–2000 to command the MIA effort there. I heard about this and started following the mission through media accounts. In 2000 Mike was succeeded in command by Lt. Col. Rennie Cory Jr., my mentor and friend at Joint Task Force Six at Fort Bliss, Texas, where we ran counterdrug operations. Tragically on April 7, 2001, in Quang Binh province, Rennie, along with his replacement, Lt. Col. George D. "Marty" Martin, five other servicemen from the Hanoi detachment, and nine Vietnamese officers were killed when their helicopter flew into a mountain in the fog. Lt. Col. John "J. T." Taylor was sent to rebuild the Hanoi detachment and put the mission back on track after this tragedy. For many years "J. T." had been a friend and also my next-door neighbor when I was teaching at West Point. In 2002 Lt. Col. Steve Hawley was selected to replace "J. T." Steve and I had gone to graduate school together at Texas A&M and taught together at West Point.

My wife, Holly, had to decide whether she should go home to our family in Texas or to remain in our quarters on Carlisle Barracks while I spent the year in Vietnam. She chose to stay at Carlisle. This would be her fourth year in the same house, a rarity in the army (we had moved eleven times in twenty years). She had developed a close circle of friends, and since I had been the garrison commander, most of the post staff knew her well. I was confident she would be carefully looked after by our army family. We knew it was going to be a tough year for her; our son, Miles, a lieutenant in the 1st Infantry Division, was in Germany preparing to leave his new bride, Tina, and deploy to Iraq after New Year's. Our daughter, Dustin, a college senior, was at Texas State University and could rarely visit.

While still a war college student I spent the spring of 2003 preparing to go to Vietnam, absorbing all I could about the mission, the unit, and Southeast Asian culture and politics. I made office calls to relevant agencies and knowledgeable people in Washington, D.C., which proved extremely valuable background. My first stop was Ann Mills Griffiths, or "AMG," as she is known, the sister of an MIA navy pilot and the executive director of the National League of Families, a very powerful organization in the MIA/POW issue. Griffiths was very kind, and we had a pleasant talk. I also made very informative visits to the Defense POW/Missing Personnel Office (DPMO), which is the policy shop for the U.S. Department of Defense, and to the State Department's Asian desk.

At the end of the Vietnam War, or American War, as it is called in Hanoi, 2,585 Americans were unaccounted for in Southeast Asia (the majority in Vietnam), 500 in Laos, 80 in Cambodia, as well as a few in China. Two agencies emerged to resolve the cases of the missing personnel, the Joint Casualty Resolution Center (JCRC) and the U.S. Army Central Identification Laboratory (CIL), then in Thailand, later at Hickam Air Force Base, Hawaii. When the lab moved to Hawaii, it became CIL-HI (pronounced "sill hi") and is now the largest forensic anthropology laboratory in the world. On January 23, 1992, Joint Task Force–Full Accounting (JTF-FA) was established in Hawaii as the successor to JCRC to provide the logistics and command and control for the Central Identification Laboratory recovery teams working in Southeast Asia and to conduct archival research and analysis in resolving cases. The JTF-FA consisted of 160 people from all of the various services, as well as civilians. The task force soon established small forward detachments in the area of operations, Detachment or Det 1 in Bangkok, Thailand; Det 2 in Hanoi, Vietnam; and Det 3 in Vientiane, Laos.

When the members of Det 2 began operating in Hanoi in 1992, they were the first U.S. government representatives to return to live full time in Vietnam. When the Senate approved the normalization process in 1994, the U.S. State Department set up an interest section in the detachment compound, known as "the Ranch." The U.S. Embassy opened in Hanoi in 1996.

Joint Task Force–Full Accounting's operating charter gave the organization the mission of dealing exclusively with MIA from Southeast Asia and the Vietnam War, while the mission of the CIL-HI lab was worldwide and covered every war—there were still 78,000 missing from World War II and 8,100 from the Korean War. In October 2003, while I was in Hanoi, the two organizations, JTF-FA and CIL-HI, merged into the 425-strong Joint POW/MIA Accounting Command (JPAC), which assumed a worldwide mission.

When I arrived in Hanoi in June 2003, 1,428 Americans in Vietnam were still unaccounted for. Since 1973 four hundred sets of remains had been repatriated by the Vietnamese, and another three hundred found by recovery teams. Of the 1,428 we were looking for in Vietnam we had little or no information on 600 cases, many of whom were pilots who went down in the South China Sea.

Recovery operations in Vietnam are conducted during thirty-day joint field activities (JFAs) four or five times a year. Normally five recovery teams (RTs) of ten to twelve persons and a ten-person investigative team (IT) arrive from Hawaii, work for a month, and return to home base at Hickam Field. The investigative team members are like scouts since they travel to fifteen or twenty sites to interview witnesses, make surveys, look for evidence, and try to determine whether a site is feasible for a future recovery operation. Each of the five recovery teams travels to its preassigned site and begins digging. The recovery team leader—an experienced army, marine, or air force captain—hires up to one hundred local Vietnamese for the heavy labor of digging, building base camps, screening dirt, and clearing jungle. Along with these teams comes a small two- or three-person research and investigative team (RIT). The RIT was composed of specialized linguists and scholars who were trying to resolve the thirty-two special cases of last known alive (LKA), Americans who were known to be alive after their capture or crash but were never accounted for by the Vietnamese government.

The mission of the commander of Detachment 2 in Hanoi, my assignment, is to wear three hats. As chief of the U.S. MIA Office, he conducts detailed technical negotiations with the Vietnamese government and has a seat on the U.S. Embassy country team. Second, as the commander of the joint field activity he is responsible for organizing the operation; receiving, commanding, and controlling the teams; providing logistics and transportation; ironing out issues with the Vietnamese central government in Hanoi; and keeping the U.S. ambassador informed and advised. Third, as Det 2 commander he is responsible for supervising the small permanent detachment in Hanoi whose members do most of the planning and support. Per bilateral agreement the Hanoi detachment is limited to seven full-time U.S. members: the commander; the deputy commander or executive officer, usually a major; an operations sergeant; an administrative sergeant; a civilian casualty resolution specialist; a civilian logistics officer; and a civilian Vietnamese interpreter.

When remains are recovered, they first go to Hanoi, where Vietnamese forensic specialists join their American counterparts from the CIL-HI lab to conduct a joint forensic review (JFR) to ensure that all repatriated remains are in fact Western in origin. When that is complete, Detachment 2 conducts a formal repatriation ceremony either at Hanoi's Noi Bai Airport or at the Da Nang Airport, and the flag-draped transfer cases are loaded onto a U.S. military aircraft and flown to Hawaii, where the identification process begins in the CIL lab.

One more statistic constantly lingered in my mind and cast a background shadow on that entire year. The number is not solid but is a reasonable best guess that the Vietnamese have about 300,000 missing and unaccounted for from the war.

This then is my tale, a personal memoir of a time and a place, memory aided mostly through my e-mails, letters, and journal entries. It, of course, is not the whole tale, for one will never know, understand, or be able to tell the whole story of what occurred in Vietnam, a place of shadows within shadows, secrets within secrets.

Chapter 1
TO THE FAR SHORE

RUMPLED AND WITH A serious case of jet lag after the long flight from Carlisle, Pennsylvania, I drove my government-rate, rented roller skate through light Sunday traffic and parked under the breezy palms of the Waikiki Hilton, where I stayed for two days while in-processing with the headquarters in late June 2003. The last time I pushed my toes into the ivory sands of Waikiki Beach, we were still at war in Vietnam. I stood on the beach for a while thinking not of Vietnam but of this new war in Iraq and of my son, Miles, who was completing his officer basic training and would in a month join his army brigade in Germany, 3rd Brigade of the 1st Infantry Division—the Big Red One, no doubt soon destined for battle.

I spent the next two days at the headquarters of Joint Task Force–Full Accounting, located at Camp Smith, on the northwest part of Honolulu. In the process I made two great new friends. The first stop and first friend was Major "Big Tim" Orner, the S4, or logistics officer. Since we were not allowed to operate in military uniform in Vietnam and could bring in very little U.S. Army equipment, Tim led me to the task force store he had set up with the best available commercial gear, such as REI, Blackhawk, Camelback, and Columbia. It was like shopping at Cabela's for free. He gave me two large transport boxes to fill, and I tossed in Gore-Tex jackets, rainsuits, gloves, boots, Camelback water kits and packs, mosquito nets, and an entire range of other gear that would make living in the jungle a little more comfortable. Tim would ship the boxes to me on the next team flight headed for Vietnam.

The second new friend was Lt. Col. Jay George, the S3, or operations officer. Jay was a wiry, quick-witted soldier with a sensible, pragmatic approach to the complexities of organizing multiple simultaneous missions. Jay and I had a long talk about the best methods of operating in Vietnam and dealing with the government. These conversations greatly boosted my confidence in being able to successfully command the Hanoi detachment.

For the remainder of two days I visited each section of the task force, preferring informal conversations to formal briefings. My view of the mission evolved considerably, becoming much more political and complicated than I had ever imagined—it seemed that each section that in-briefed me clearly had its own spin on the issues.

In addition, I learned that my old friend, who was also the guy I was replacing, Lt. Col. Steve Hawley, was going to be a hard act to follow as Det 2 commander. It was clear he had done great work, made some important innovations, and had pushed very hard. I was gratified, too, to learn that Lt. Col. J. T. Taylor, another old friend and Steve's predecessor, was considered to have been a very effective detachment commander because of his simple, decent, modest, respectful, and friendly treatment of everyone he encountered on both sides. I decided that he was the model I wanted to adopt.

I thought the staff seemed somewhat surprised by my depth of knowledge of the background issues, the diplomacy, and the details of specific cases. Unlike all the other detachment commanders, who had rolled straight out of battalion command with little time to do more than pack and go to Hanoi, I had the advantage of ten months as a war college student and the leisure to do plenty of research on the task force, the mission, and Vietnam. I felt very well armed intellectually for the challenge ahead.

I discovered that people in Pacific Command seemed to have a unique concept of time and distance. As part of their job they dashed across six or eight time zones for a quick meeting and back. My new boss, the commanding general of JTF-FA, Brigadier General Steve Redmann, would just leave for Washington, D.C., six time zones east, and then would come straight back in a few days, followed by a quick visit with me in Hanoi, twelve time zones west of D.C., then six time zones back east to Hawaii. No wonder these people fell asleep at meetings and no one even noticed.

After a few informative days at the headquarters in Honolulu, I launched on a twenty-hour trip to Bangkok. It was apparently a rule that you can't go to Southeast Asia without spending six or seven hours on layover at Tokyo's Narita Airport, which is the same distance from Hawaii as a direct flight to

Bangkok, so it doubles the trip distance. It had something to do with the government contract, which also recently ended business-class travel for the government, so everyone flew economy class.

I arrived at Bangkok's Suvarnabhumi Airport near midnight, breezed through customs by waving my black diplomatic passport, and was met at the exit by the operations sergeant of the Bangkok detachment, who promptly drove me to my hotel for much-needed sleep. My three heavy bags simply evaporated from the lobby as I checked in with an exquisite Thai hostess, who escorted me to my suite, where my luggage awaited me. Even in my blurry state I realized I had transcended into a new universe, my first experience as an oriental raja.

The Cathay Pacific flight the next morning was too short to take full advantage of the Chinese standard of service and luxury. I suspected that traveling around Asia on oriental airlines was going to ruin me and that I would forever after have nothing but disdain for American carriers, a notion that was solidly confirmed when I returned home to the States.

Approaching Hanoi's Noi Bai Airport, I could see the imposing profile of Tam Dao Mountain in the distance, its upper peaks bathed in a soft summer shower. During the war the mountain, nicknamed "Thud Ridge," served as a navigation point for American pilots flying missions to Hanoi, not Hanoi proper, but the railyards north of the city. Hanoi itself was bombed but once during the war, an air force accident. Looking down through the aircraft window, I tried to imagine what it must have been like for those brave pilots, threading a sky full of surface-to-air missiles and antiaircraft fire. Tam Dao Mountain is measled with crash sites.

Oriental royalty or not, one did not simply wave a black diplomatic passport and whisk through Vietnamese customs. First, there was the line where arriving passengers turned in a lengthy health form and received a cursory inspection by medical personnel. At the diplomatic desk a teenager, polite but vigilant and wearing a security uniform, carefully scrutinized my passport and my visa. Finally, with a resounding thump, he officially stamped me into country and waved me onward.

It wasn't hard to spot Lt. Col. Steve Hawley. At six feet six he towered over the crowd of tiny people waiting to meet other passengers. For the first time I shook hands with Mr. Dang Van Thinh, my driver. Bowing to show proper respect and taking my hand with his right, he gently covered the back of my hand with his left in the Vietnamese fashion. He had clear sparkling eyes, a ready smile, and a decent command of English. We would eventually spend countless hours and miles together sharing the extreme dangers of the Vietnamese roads.

The forty-five-minute drive into Hanoi to the detachment compound carried us past lush green rice paddies, scores of brightly colored farmers bent double in the blazing sun while carefully tending the lifeblood of their nation. I rolled down the window and inhaled the very distinctive aroma of Asia—peanut oil and fried rice, fish and water buffalo dung, charcoal smoke, blue plumes spitting from legions of motorbikes, the thick scent of a land smothered in tropical vines and leaves. I felt a sense of complete serenity, a sense of place. I had anchored at last upon the far shore.

Chapter 2
TAPHONOMICS

THE LONG, SHADED BOULEVARDS and French colonial architecture of Hanoi give it a languid character, one contradicted by the tide of honking motorbikes flooding the major streets. I know the streets of Berlin, Sydney, London, Prague, Florence, Manila, and even Beijing but had never been captured so quickly by a city.

I spent but a few nights at "the Ranch," as the detachment compound was known, the former home of the Cuban embassy. Steve Hawley and I took off almost immediately for my right-seat ride, or reconnaissance trip, and then returned and changed command. Just after the change of command the entire detachment would relocate to new quarters in the upscale foreign district called Tay Ho, or West Lake.

The next afternoon, after a meet-and-greet lunch with Ray Porter, the deputy chief of mission, or DCM, the embassy's second in command, Steve Hawley, William "Buddy" Newell, and I caught a Vietnam Air flight that took us eleven hundred kilometers south to Ho Chi Minh City (HCMC), still called Saigon by the South Vietnamese.

After a night at the elegant Caravelle Hotel, famous during the war for its rooftop bar, where reporters wrote their dispatches, we journeyed southeast by van to the very tip of the Mekong Delta near Vung Tau. A short ride in a single-engine, Russian-made MI-8 helicopter took us to a recovery site in the middle of a vast mangrove swamp. The whole operation was built on bamboo platforms above the swamp and was worked like a marine salvage project with coffer dams, dikes, and water pumps. The workers came in by boat, and all of the material and the anthropology crew were flown in each

"The Ranch," Doc Ngu Street, Ba Dinh district, the Hanoi home of Det 2, JTF-FA, 1992–2003, was the former Cuban Embassy compound.

day from Vung Tau, where they lived in a fleabag hotel. The conditions in the swamp were harsh—too unhealthy to set up a typical base camp. The site anthropologist was Dr. Pete Miller, a longtime veteran of recovery operations and a specialist in wet sites. Although the other teams at various recovery sites were wrapping up their mission and getting ready to meet in Da Nang before returning to Hawaii, we had received permission from the Vietnamese to extend the stay of Pete's team until it finished the site, probably several more weeks.

From there we went six hundred kilometers north to Hue, where we then flew west in a twin-engine MI-17 to the A Shau valley, to a site on a mountain nearly touching the border with Laos. Hamburger Hill (Apbia Mountain) was just to our north. Western Thua Thien–Hue province is about a thousand square miles of mountainous, triple-canopy jungle as remote and sparsely populated as the bottom of the ocean. Our helicopter seemed the size of a flea, a pitiful little lifeboat on a vast green sea.

We spent the night in a pretty good base camp the team had built on the mountain. Everything had to be elevated on bamboo platforms to keep us above the black leeches and five kinds of poisonous snakes. The shelter was double tarped against the terrific rainstorms and had excellent mosquito netting to guard against the notoriously vile strain of malaria common to the region.

Landing in Hanoi the next afternoon, I stripped off my filthy field gear and an hour later was at an embassy cocktail party. It was a nice affair, but I would rather have been back on top of that mountain in the A Shau.

Mountain base camp above the A Shau Valley near the Lao border.

Landing zone to support the A Shau Valley site, twin-engine MI-17 landing. Buddy Newell is sitting on the log.

Screening station, A Shau Valley site. American team member taking a final look before the Vietnamese screener dumps the debris.

This shot of the screening station shows the forbidding terrain of western Thua Thien–Hue province.

At the 2003 Fourth of July party, the embassy chief of counsel (in charge of passports, visas, and assistance to U.S. citizens) came up to Steve and me and told us that last week a young American man who was teaching English in Bangkok and a young college girl (his family friend from back home) had taken off on a motor scooter from Hanoi to visit a mountain resort up north near Sa Pa, on the Chinese border. While on the road, suddenly—like a bolt of thunder—they were swept off the road by a huge mudslide. The girl, critically injured, was found by sheer luck in a local hospital by an American tourist, who had sense enough to call the embassy. The Vietnamese, of course, had never reported her injury to anybody, especially the embassy, which evacuated the girl to a hospital in Thailand. Meanwhile, for the past week the boy's body had been missing somewhere in the mudslide or even in the river. The Vietnamese did not appear very interested in finding him, and the boy's family in the States was frantic. When the chief of counsel asked whether we could help, we said maybe.

The next morning we had a meeting with Brig. Gen. Steve Redmann, our boss, who had come for the change of command, and Ambassador Ray Burghardt. The ambassador said his first mission was to help Americans and asked whether we could attempt to find the boy's body. Most of our teams were in Da Nang, coming out of the field to go back to Hawaii, but nobody in the world knew more about finding bodies than those guys. Even though it was not our mission to find a tourist and was probably against countless army, Department of Defense, and U.S. government regulations, Brig. Gen. Redmann said we would do it. That made me even prouder to be an American.

I spent the day putting together an emergency expedition to try to recover this young man, the whole time thinking of the agony his poor parents had to be enduring. We got everything organized to fly up a team from Da Nang, and soon one of our Vietnamese government counterparts, Mr. Tran Van Tu, called and said his colleagues would have no problems with this, which was interesting because we had not told them anything about our plan. Somehow they seemed to know everything we did and said.

Just as Steve's going-away party had gotten started, the embassy called and said that the local province chief had suddenly become interested in finding the young man and, in fact, had found the body, meaning that he did not want to be embarrassed when our team went up there and did his job for him. The good thing was that the embassy realized that we in JTF-FA and Hanoi Det 2 would do the right thing, no matter what the regulations dictated, which boosted my morale.

It was a simple, traditional change-of-command ceremony in the foyer of "the Ranch" compound. Steve passed the detachment guidon to Brig. Gen. Redmann, who passed it on to me, and we followed with short speeches. Afterward I spent some time touring around Hanoi with Brig. Gen. Redmann, his wife, Pat, and daughter, Kate, who had just graduated from high school and was headed for college in Virginia. I enjoyed their company. They were a bright and interesting family, and the ladies were very sweet to me. We went to a very long lunch with Ambassador and Mrs. Burghardt at their quarters and then to a party at the home of the defense attaché, Col. Steve Ball and his wife, Allaine, a beautiful residence out in Tay Ho district.

The next morning I moved all of my gear over to the new detachment building, also in Tay Ho, and right on the lake. I had a nice, two-bedroom apartment with a grand view of the lake and was happier for my team, who had much better quarters than at the old compound. We had two large, adjacent buildings with offices on the lower floors and apartments above, as well as a glassed-in bar on the roof, with one of the best views of the city.

I was very quickly getting attuned to the pasha lifestyle a well-resourced Westerner enjoys in developing Asia, though I did not yet understand that it would be offset by exhausting, steaming-wet days in the jungle. I was used to commanding and leading large organizations, but this was a new experience. The Vietnamese administrative staff, house girls, and drivers were very sensitive to even my slightest hint. If I mentioned that I needed to go someplace, like magic one of our fleet of Pajero SUVs would suddenly appear. I also learned that these employees are perhaps too sensitive. The cook, Ms. Tam, once became very upset because I had crossed breakfast off of my meal list the day before. It took two different interpreters to convince her that I did not hate her breakfast and was not going to fire her; I had simply decided not to eat because an hour after breakfast we were going to have French pastry at the change of command, and I did not want to overeat.

The Vietnamese are very lovely and mild people, but they wear their hearts on their sleeve. My face eventually hurt from smiling continually because, if I was preoccupied and walked past the staff while wearing my "thinking frown," they took it as a message that they were headed for the chopping block.

For part of the day, Brig. Gen. Redmann and I were in meetings with Vietnamese officials in my counterpart's office, called the Vietnamese Office for Seeking Missing Persons (VNOSMP), which is a division of their Americas Department of the Ministry of Foreign Affairs, similar to our State Department. We had to iron out difficult issues, which meant some extremely polite talk and many compliments and smiles, while the main points and disagreements were simply slipped in offhandedly, almost as an unimportant afterthought. The Vietnamese are very tough and wily in negotiations, but the experience at the table is very interesting because nobody gets upset or raises a voice; their faces take on a sad look, and they express the deepest regret that they cannot help out their dear American friends because the big boss would never agree. Of course, there is no big boss; they themselves are the big boss. Nonetheless, I came to greatly admire and actually like several of them.

But then, driving back to our detachment we saw a Ministry of Public Security goon on a street corner approach an illegal street vender and enforce the "no-selling" law on Hang Dau street by slapping her to the ground and scattering her mangoes in the traffic. I tried to convince my driver, Mr. Thinh, to run over the security guy with the Pajero, but Buddy, my interpreter, calmed me down. Buddy explained to me that the city spent a great deal of effort organizing licensed markets and lost revenue to the illegal street vendors.

I discovered that the child safety drill in Vietnam involves the mother's getting a good grip on her babies and her baskets as she rides on the back of a

The Furama Hotel, near China Beach, Da Nang.

motorbike driven by her husband, who hurriedly weaves in and out of traffic. Hanoi has nearly a million people, about the size of San Antonio. During my stay I counted four traffic lights.

Hanoi's Noi Bai airport was surprisingly clean, modern, and efficient, although "smoke free" was not a concept practiced in Vietnam. Buddy and I boarded an afternoon Vietnam Air flight to spend a week in Da Nang. where all of the teams were gathering to write their reports before going back to Hawaii. We had excavated five sites and would bring home three lost sons as a result of this joint field activity. When the teams departed, we would fly down to the Mekong Delta to close out the site we had extended for ten days—until the end of July 2003. As we were landing in Da Nang, I realized the commercial airport was the old U.S. base; the Vikings' squadron logo was still faintly visible on one of the hangars on the left side of the runway. The Vikings were a navy propeller squadron that flew mail and passengers back and forth from the beach to the Seventh Fleet offshore, and I myself flew on one of their aircraft in 1970. I asked Buddy whether I could go over to the hangar and see it again, but he said that that part of the airport was a Mig base and thus forbidden.

The detachment field headquarters in Da Nang was a series of rooms at government rate in the Furama Resort, on the northern reaches of China Beach. I was the *Ông*, "The Mr.," or big boss, so the Furama gave us a nice, fussy reception.

While waiting for the reports to start arriving, Buddy Newell and I went exploring. We went down to Ngu Hanh Son (Marble Mountain) a few kilometers south, where we climbed through the old Viet Cong cave stronghold. In one part, the ladder went nearly two hundred feet straight up to a lookout or outpost in the side of the mountain. Needless to say, it did not meet OSHA safety standards, but we were careful and helped each other past the parts where all of the railing had rusted away. Several small Vietnamese children in flip-flops passed me on the way up, but they were nice and offered to help me. I had learned to say in Vietnamese, "Go away from me, rude child with no respect for your elders."

Because I was determined to learn enough Vietnamese to get around on my own, every day either Buddy or Mr. Thinh, the driver, would teach me new words. Vietnamese is a tonal language with a half-dozen sounds for the letter "a" alone. After a few weeks I felt confident enough to order lunch for Buddy and me. We had the red underwear chicken and an umbrella, plus two shovels to drink.

In Da Nang I finally got a chance to meet the majority of folks in my command, minus the several hundred Vietnamese who worked for us at the dig sites. My training as a garrison commander came in handy on the first day as I gave at least five speeches to different teams and events and actually performed a promotion. Chief Warrant Officer Two Flores made his Chief Warrant Officer Three, and Hawaii faxed his orders. As far as anyone could tell, it was a historic occasion, the first field promotion done in Vietnam since the war. We had no chief warrant officer three bars to pin on Flores, so at the last minute I decided to take two pieces of green hundred-mile-an-hour tape and to blacken in three stripes with a pen. It surprised everyone when I pulled them out and stuck them on his shirt. Flores later told me that he collected historic warrant officer insignia and that the homemade stripes and the occasion made them his most important memorabilia.

I have always sort of "collected" eccentrics, but I had to admit that my collection would simply overload with most of the teams under one roof. I do not think I have ever met in one place so many extraordinarily interesting and decidedly different individuals.

I spent the evening with the science guys, the forensic anthropologists who are assigned to each team and who manage the excavations. Their dean was the legendary Dr. C. Elliot Moore II, or "Hoss," who had been doing recovery operations for more than a decade. A six-foot-four Kansas cowboy, complete with Tony Llama boots, huge Texas straw hat, and Cambodian

Dr. C. Elliott "Hoss" Moore II.

scarf, Hoss was completely deaf but a good lip reader in several languages, as well as one of fifty board-certified forensic anthropologists in the United States. He became an immediate fast friend and afterward greeted me with a bear hug. I always tried to take Hoss to dinner when he came in country, and I would listen to his incredible stories of past recovery operations. We usually went to Western eateries, where Hoss, being deaf, told his tales in a broad voice that carried across the restaurant. The place never failed to grow quiet as many of the customers put down their silverware and leaned toward his voice as the tales spun out. "Am I talking too loud?" he would ask me. "No, Hoss," I always replied, "you're talking just fine."

The anthropologists, or anthros, as we called them, spent the evening drinking beer and arguing passionately about the subtleties of taphonomic erosion. I let this go on for a half-hour before asking what taphonomic meant. After a fascinating lecture I learned it means the science of how various soils and environmental conditions degrade and transport biological material, in this case the eroding bones of our missing boys. Involved in this effort were all sorts of unexploded ordnance specialists, metallurgists, field medicine doctors, medics, linguists, intelligence analysts, team leaders, mortuary affairs specialists, and the life support crew.

The life support analysts, or LSAs, are probably the most uniquely trained folks in the entire military. Their job is to recognize or research and identify any and all equipment and parts associated with dozens of variations of ejection seats, survival equipment, parachutes, or flight gear issued to military pilots between 1958 and 1973. They can sometimes look at a single scrap of harness or even a washer or grommet, dive into their field computer databases and chemistry sets, and usually within a few hours tell you what type of aircraft the object came from and what years it was used. The more I saw of the high-quality fieldwork, the talent, the dedication, and the hardships the teams endured to complete their mission, the more humbled I became by the privilege of command.

During the three or four days of writing, it was my duty to sign all of the twenty or so accounts generated. There would be one lengthy report about each of the five excavation sites, as well as shorter ones on the fifteen or so sites the investigative team visited. It was a little like grading papers when I taught military history at West Point. One of my most important responsibilities was to review and approve the field reports written by folks who had been doing this work for years. The reports are public documents, so my job was to make sure they would make sense and could be understood by the families of the missing (believe me, they read them all), by Congress, and by the half-dozen special-interest groups in Washington who make their living on the POW/MIA issue. In an odd way it was the right system in that if the least experienced, lowest common denominator—which would be me—could understand these accounts, then everybody else could as well.

I very quickly got an education in the various types and complexities of excavation-and-recovery operations. There are four basic types of recovery sites: straightforward crash site; crash with burial; ground loss with isolated burial; and ground loss incident without burial.

The simplest to work and which perhaps also offered the best chance of finding remains is a straightforward crash site. Although there is almost never a complete wreckage because the locals have long ago salvaged the metal, usually enough scattered fragments remain to enable verification of the type of aircraft, and, with any luck, the exact aircraft by means of a data plate or a serial number on a part. During the war, more than two thousand aircraft were lost, and in the majority of these cases either the crew was rescued, or they were killed and their bodies recovered, or they were captured and later released. Around three hundred crash sites are associated with the various MIAs, so it is important to try to determine whether the aircraft in question is actually the one associated with a particular case. One area in the north, above Hanoi, has six or seven crash sites within ten kilometers of each other, including four F-4 Phantoms, but only one site is associated with an MIA.

Once a team is reasonably certain it has the right aircraft, the next big step is to try to determine whether the crew was still in it when it crashed. The team searches for life support evidence such as ejection seat parts, parachute parts, survival kit fragments—anything that will indicate to the life support analysts whether anyone was still aboard at impact.

If there is a good possibility the crew stayed aboard, the size of the dig is determined by the debris field. Some sites are huge and require many return trips to find the area with a concentration of cockpit parts. In the case of a straight crash, chances of finding bones or teeth within or just under the debris field are good. Of course, the easy sites have already been examined, which means the remainder of the known sites are in challenging locations such as steep mountain slopes or the base of sheer cliffs.

In a crash with burial site, the conditions are the same except that the locals buried the remains of the crew or what remains they could find. The Vietnamese are very superstitious or perhaps sensitive about human bodies, even that of a dead American. This type of case becomes more problematic because, if eyewitnesses are still alive, they are aging and therefore struggle with pinpointing the location of an event that occurred three decades ago. Even more unreliable are secondhand witnesses, such as a well-meaning young person who offers to show the team where his uncle once showed him—ten years ago—the burial spot of an American pilot who died twenty years before that. Of course, there are also suspected cases of witnesses deliberately misleading the team members so they will keep coming back and hiring locals to work for them.

A ground loss incident without burial is a situation in which one or more Americans die, perhaps in a firefight, and their bodies are left behind and unburied. A recovery team has a good chance of retrieving enough remains to extract a DNA sample if animals or the force of taphonomic erosion into a streambed has not completely scattered the remains.

The toughest sites are ground loss with isolated burial, in which, for example, a pilot parachutes but dies and is buried under a tree in the jungle. Another example would be a POW who is going up the Ho Chi Minh Trail, gets sick and dies, and is buried beside the path. Recovery in this case is entirely dependent on a reliable witness, a good landmark, and lots of luck.

Adding to this complexity of types of recovery operations are many and various site conditions. Wet sites such as streams, swamps, ponds, and rice paddies have to be dammed and drained with a series of pumps. Dry sites are easier but might be on a thirty-degree slope of a mountain, where the team literally has to tie off to trees. Also, rockfall is always a danger on slope sites. Other combinations of conditions, such as access permission, present additional hurdles. Vietnam has a considerable number of militarily sensitive areas, as is the case in any country. Some sites are so remote as to require the team to build and live in a base camp for the entire dig. If a hotel site—a site where the team can live in a village guest house or nearby hotel—is available, it becomes either a "drive site" or a "fly site." Flying in and out daily by helicopter is a risk because a team could lose half of its "dig days" waiting for the weather to clear enough to fly. Drive sites were the best from my point of view as the detachment commander because the team could live fairly comfortably in a guest house without the health and accident dangers inherent in a base camp. Moreover, driving is more reliable than flying, although it is probably just as dangerous, considering the poor condition of Vietnamese roads and the chaotic traffic.

After five days in Da Nang I fell into solitary brooding about this newfound knowledge, which brought to mind the Japanese word *koran,* the compelling, unsolvable type of trite Zen riddles such as "one hand clapping" or "the noise of a single tree falling," confirmation that I had arrived in a new world. Life as I had known it before now suddenly had little relevance.

Chapter 3
LA RUE SANS JOIE

CLOSING OUT THE SEVENTY-FOURTH joint field activity, I gained my first true sense of the mature patience required not only to conduct the actual field science of an MIA recovery but also to endure the glacial pace of the very deliberate process of identification and family notification. Captain Shawn "Zeke" Zukowsky and Dr. "Hoss" Moore gave me a final overview of their work on case 0248, a very successful recovery. In this case the remains of USAF Major James L. Carter of Pasadena, California, Sergeant Edward M. Parsley from Naugatuck, West Virginia, and Sergeant Therman M. Waller from Wynne, Arkansas, were recovered from a crash site in Quang Tri province near Dong Ha.

Major Carter and crew in a C-123 Provider of the 311th Cargo Squadron were flying a three-leg supply mission, Da Nang–Khe Sanh–Dong Ha, on February 3, 1966, when the aircraft inexplicably crashed into a mountain. Twenty-five search-and-rescue missions looked for the aircraft without success, while local villagers buried the crew's remains. Between 2000 and 2004 JTF-FA conducted five recovery operations. Neither Zeke, Hoss, the recovery crew, nor I had any way to know the outcome at that time, but the identification was completed by CIL nine months later, in June 2004, and the families were notified, and the remains buried almost twenty months later, in June 2005. Carter and Parsley were buried in Arlington National Cemetery, and Waller was interred in the Missouri Veterans Cemetery in Bloomfield, Missouri. I learned very quickly that I needed to be ever mindful of the long view.

With Mr. Thinh driving, Buddy and I went to the Da Nang Airport to load a commercial charter with the eighty recovery team members, who were on their way back to Hawaii, where they would stay until the next joint field activity. Then the giant U.S. Air Force C-17 lumbered in to take away their equipment. We loaded all of the team gear while watching a half-dozen Vietnamese Mig fighter jets take off and spin upward in a roar, putting on quite an air show to impress their American counterparts. The only time I ever saw the Migs flying in Da Nang was when a U.S. Air Force plane was on the tarmac. Loading completed, Buddy and I watched the C-17 roll halfway down the runway when cockpit computer bells and whistles apparently went off, announcing that this was not a very good time to fly.

God bless the pilot, he tried to take off twice, meaning he could spend the night in Thailand if he could get airborne; he certainly gave it his best effort. The result was my very own attached C-17 crew at the Furama Resort at China Beach, along with a giant, nonflyable U.S. aircraft full of very sensitive navigation and communication gear that we could never let anybody else see. Fortunately, these birds carried two Ravens—USAF special security types—who spent the next few days in the plane on the Da Nang runway, while the pilots and crew lounged in the swimming pool, except those at China Beach.

They were nice folks, but they were reservists. Also at this time I had to close out the extended site, so I needed to leave the next morning for Vung Tau, down near the Mekong Delta and in the middle of a mangrove swamp. Because of this, I collected our part-time brethren and gave them a detailed in-brief about hazards for the unwary in Vietnam, hoping to scare them enough so they would not venture beyond the hotel compound.

Teams unloading their gear at Da Nang Airport.

U.S. Air Force C-17 loads the teams' gear at Da Nang Airport.

Hai Van Pass, Route 1, *La rue sans joie* (Street without Joy) at the old French fort north of Da Nang.

That afternoon, with faithful Thinh at the wheel, Buddy and I headed north up Route 1 to Hai Van Pass and back. Route 1, the legendary road from Saigon, runs nearly a thousand coastal miles to Hanoi and is the centerpiece of Bernard Fall's book *Street without Joy,* or *La rue sans joie,* as the French soldiers called it. Hai Van Pass is a chokepoint dividing Vietnam, equally famous for its remarkable beauty and its old French fortifications. We enjoyed the vista stretching all the way to China Beach and Monkey Mountain and explored every inch of the overgrown French fort, keeping a keen eye out for hissing cobras and slithering kraits. As sunset approached, we scrambled the twenty miles back to Da Nang, avoiding the adventure of Route 1 in the dark. For the next year much of my life became intertwined with Route 1 and its many facets and faces.

The next morning Buddy and I headed for Saigon, leaving behind Daniel Young, our brilliant logistics officer, to babysit the C-17 crew and their broken airplane. Landing at Tan Son Nhat Airport on the outskirts of Ho Chi Minh City, I decided Saigon reminded me of Los Angeles. Saigon was to LA as Hanoi was to San Antonio, and I had never cared much for LA. We spent part of the afternoon at the War Remembrance Museum, which used to be called the American War Crimes Museum until the Vietnamese decided they needed the United States as a sponsor to help them get admitted into the World Trade Organization.

The museum was essentially an unapologetic propaganda showcase of revised history and reinterpreted photographs. Many Americans become upset with the displays, but, as a realist and a historian, I know that the victors get to write the past as they wish. While there, at a little vendor booth, I discovered one of my favorite field scarves, or "drive-on rag," as it was known in the old days.

Almost everyone in the recovery teams adopts a distinctive scarf; some have bright-colored Cambodian ones, some pastel Lao, while others prefer patterns from obscure mountain tribes or scarves with Thai, Chinese, and Indonesian designs. It becomes a sort of badge and a topic of conversation: Where did you get it? How much did it cost? What's the story behind it? This particular scarf had a black-and-white check and a single red stripe across the bottom, a Viet Cong battle scarf, a symbol of the guerrilla underdogs, who were defeated by the Americans in Tet '68. The guerrillas were rounded up, jailed, murdered, scattered, and disenfranchised by their victorious North Vietnamese brothers and allies, who saw them as a potential threat to northern rule. Theirs is one of the unspoken histories in Vietnam. In a symbolic way I saw the scarf as an American statement: always for the underdog.

After a comfortable night in the Caravelle Hotel, we drove several hours to the old French port of Vung Tau, where an arm of the Saigon River dumps into the South China Sea. There we checked in to the team's fleabag hotel, called the Royale. Before we boarded the single-engine MI-8 helicopter to fly out to the site, I took steps to defeat the pesky rats in my room by carefully sealing up the food I had brought in a strong plastic container. Buddy just shook his head and muttered, "The colonels I've known usually don't waste their time; these are Vietnamese rats." The rats, of course, made short work of the container after we left.

The sheer vastness of the Mekong mangrove swamp struck me as we flew low above the snarled trees; it was a steaming wet, ominous version of western Thua Thien–Hue province. The case in question was the crash site of U.S. Marine Corps Capt. Carl Edwin Long, from Dallas and the Texas A&M class of 1966.

On December 20, 1969, Captain Long and USN Lt. (jg) Joel A. Sandberg were flying a propeller-driven OV-10 Bronco out of Vung Tau as part of the U.S. Navy Light Attack Squadron Four (VAL-4), "Black Ponies" Rung Sat special patrol, to spot Viet Cong positions in the delta. Long was checking out a suspicious sampan in the Long Tau shipping channel when his wingman reported he had lost radio contact with Long. Long's aircraft was spotted in the swamp, and an attempt was made to hook it to a CH-47 Chinook helicopter. Unfortunately, the lifting strap broke, and the aircraft sank into the morass before Long's body could be pulled from the cockpit.

Thirty-four years later the investigative team questioned a shrimp farmer who was raising shrimp in a canal near the reported crash site. The farmer said he had been living there for only twenty years and knew nothing of the crash. However, he mentioned a place out in the mangrove, where the undergrowth was not very thick, and oil bubbled up to the surface. Buddy, Steve Hawley, my predecessor, and Dr. Pete Miller, a wet-site specialist, took a boat and then canoes to the site and decided the dig was just about feasible.

Miller and his team, led by Capt. Geoff Kent, and about two hundred Vietnamese workers spent seventy-one days clearing vegetation, building two square coffer dams, one inside the other, draining the site into the delta and well away from the shrimp farm to avoid environmental issues with the farmer. They constructed a bamboo bridge several hundred feet long from the site to the only dry ground available, the ten-foot-wide banks of the canal, where they set up the work and screening stations. It was a task of monumental proportions in an incredibly unforgiving environment. I was simply astonished the first time I saw it.

The MI-8 gingerly set its wheels on three small, wooden platforms rising out of the muck. As we hopped out, we were met by a smiling Captain Kent, who greeted us with "Sir, we got the gold." Crossing the rickety bamboo

Delta dig site, marked by square.

Delta recovery site: an engine and propeller of Capt. Carl Long's OV-10 Bronco in the foreground.

Capt. Geoff Kent, recovery team leader, minding pumps draining the delta recovery site.

bridge to the coffer dams, I could see in the wide, deep pit pieces of wing, engines with bent propeller blades, rocket pods, and scattered aircraft parts. The team had dug about twelve feet below the original surface with a series of stairstep levels shorn up by the strong marine plywood we had imported from Hawaii. Cave-in was a constant danger.

Knowing that I had gone to graduate school at Texas A&M and that many of my family members were Aggies, Geoff held out his closed fist and said, "Here you go, sir. Gig 'em!" He then dropped Carl Long's Class of '66 ring in my palm. I held the ring for a long time, wanting to get on my cell phone and call Long's parents, as well as Col. Sam Hawes, my oldest army and Aggie buddy, but I could not tell anyone. The news had to be kept a complete secret until the official ID was made at the CIL-HI lab and the Marine Corps had notified the family. I held the ring a long while and then walked off down the canal path so the others would not see my tears.

On September 16, 2004, USMC Capt. Carl Edwin Long was buried in Arlington National Cemetery.

Instead of driving back to Ho Chi Minh City, Buddy got the bright idea to take the Vung Tau–Saigon hydrofoil for the forty-mile trip up the Saigon River. For an hour we enjoyed a wonderful view of the river and an assortment of birds, as well as head-on close-ups of a competing company's boats charging at us at an alarming closure rate. The Vietnamese are very competitive people, as are the hydrofoil captains, who have a habit of playing "chicken" on the river with the other boats. This is an exciting experience for the first-class passengers, who are directly in the bow with an unobstructed

USMC Capt. Carl Long's Texas Aggie Ring, Class of '66.

Down in the delta, waiting for the taxi.
Courtesy Buddy Newell

Delta taxi.

view of the near-death experience. Actually, two hydros had collided the previous week, although no one in Saigon was surprised; the accident was only a matter of time. Fortunately, no serious injuries occurred, and the incident had thankfully made the boat captains somewhat more cautious, for they cleared each other by a good ten feet.

I arrived back in Hanoi to find that the four-by-six-foot crate I was allowed to ship from the States had been delivered; in it was all of the stuff I

Vung Tau–Saigon hydrofoil, Saigon River.

needed, and everything was in perfect condition. My wife, Holly, and I had spent a great deal of time deciding what to put in the crate, and it turned out that we had made a number of wise choices. I hugged my mountain bike and all ten packs of razor blades, played "Buena Vista Social Club" on the stereo, and danced around the office with a Dr. Pepper in each hand. All thirteen boxes inside were like Christmas even though I planned to give most of the food away as gifts.

Sergeant Urbano Galindo, from El Paso, who was at the detachment for a few weeks helping with equipment, quickly showed up at my door with a smile on his face. His hobby was Tex-Mex cooking, and he knew I had shipped a couple of pounds of pinto beans, salsa, and tortillas. We had a very long and serious conversation about how he was going to cook the frijoles the next week when he returned from Hue.

Then the phone rang, and on the other end was Major Tom Dicken, our marine deputy detachment commander, whom I had sent to Da Nang to help Daniel Young babysit the broken C-17. The aircraft was repaired and gone, but Tom said a South African contractor who was building a road had told him that his bulldozers had just turned up a skull, part of a jawbone, and partially burned U.S. Air Force papers from the war.

Keith Gary Flanagan, our casualty resolution chief, and I immediately packed our bags to fly back to Da Nang. Fortunately, anthropologist Pete Miller was still in country, closing the site at Vung Tau. I asked him to bring his team sergeant, his explosive ordnance disposal (EOD) sergeant, and a linguist and meet us in Da Nang to do the contingency operation. Buddy called the VNOSMP and explained the situation to Mr. Tran Van Tu, who agreed to the mission and said that we could work out the details with the district chief and the local military commander when we got to Da Nang.

Later in the morning I got a call from Ron Ward, who was the boss of the research and investigative team (RIT). He and Master Sergeant Kelly Ray had been in Hanoi for a few weeks at the National Library, trying to piece together the details of Group 559, the North Vietnamese Army (NVA) unit that ran the Ho Chi Minh trail during the war. Ron told me that, although they had been scheduled to interview a couple of NVA veterans, the interviews were suddenly cancelled. They were directed by Senior Colonel Key to cease research because the Vietnamese were upset over the latest U.S. House of Representatives Vietnam Human Rights amendment on the State Department's authorization bill. This legislation essentially condemned Vietnam, mainly over religious freedom. Shortly afterward, Mr. Tu informed me that Mr. Nguyen Van Dao, the head of the VNOSMP, would like to discuss this congressional resolution. I was very concerned that this political issue might also halt the contingency operation we were putting together for Da Nang.

By then the embassy was on the phone, asking us to report any fallout from the resolution, so I went to talk to the ambassador and the political section to figure out how best to respond to Mr. Dao's request for a meeting.

Nguyen Van Dao, as the head of VNOSMP, was my senior counterpart in the Vietnamese government, and in a very short time I had grown to like and respect him. He was a cool customer, very worldly and had served at the United Nations in New York and in Washington, D.C. He had an impish smile and a surfer haircut, looked people straight in the eye, and spoke perfect English, although we used interpreters for official meetings. I found out he had spent several years in Cuba and guessed he had learned Spanish, as I had growing up on the Texas border. One time at dinner, out of the blue I launched into Spanish with him. He never missed a beat. We just chatted about family matters, but all of the officials, security personnel, and interpreters around us seemed very nervous because they were not sure what we were saying. I think we both thought it was fun to make them wonder whether we were sharing state secrets.

Scott Bellard, the political counselor and acting deputy chief of mission, and I went to the VNOSMP office, located in a grand old French colonial building on Duong Dien Bien Phu Street near Ho Chi Minh's tomb. That day Mr. Dao seemed more melancholy than angry. He started in about the House resolution on human rights in Vietnam, complaining that it was like a ton of bricks falling on his head and that the people were angry at all Americans over this. I replied that, as just a simple soldier, I did not have anything to do with political matters. I suggested that he discuss it with the political section and stated that there was no connection between our humanitarian mission and that issue. He replied that he had just wanted to make sure we knew he was upset about the resolution.

The same thing would happen again in the spring of 2004, when a number of cities and states passed resolutions recognizing the Dai Nam national flag, which has the yellow background and three red stripes of the old South Vietnamese regime during the war. In pursuit of a lost cause, the political element of heavily Vietnamese communities in the States started calling it the Vietnamese Heritage and Freedom Flag. On the eve of an official visit from a delegation from Vietnam, the city of Garden Grove, California, went so far as to declare itself a "no-Communist" zone, effectively banning the Vietnamese officials from the city. As a Texan with a graveyard full of Confederate relatives, I knew all about lost causes. One Vietnamese told me in jest that Hanoi should pass a resolution recognizing the Confederate Stars and Bars and fly it from the Hanoi Opera House. This sort of politics was not helpful to my cause, which was solely to find our lost ones and bring them home.

The meeting with Mr. Dao ended on a cordial note with a parting cup of green tea. I did not bring up the Da Nang contingency mission, and he did not withdraw permission to launch it. I have never been sure whether the VNOSMP had somehow gotten its wires crossed and forgotten to tell me to halt the project or whether it was a case of deliberate, benign neglect.

The next morning, a Sunday, Gary, Pete, and I found ourselves sitting at a long table in a sweltering maintenance shed at a construction site a few kilometers west of Da Nang. Although by now I had acquired a good bit of experience dealing with high party officials in Hanoi, this was my first site negotiation with local leaders. The village chief, the hamlet head, the district boss, and the province representative were all at the table. The *dia-wi,* or captain, who was the local military commander, had even put on his uniform. It took a good while to first visit and then get down to business. Everybody at the table had to have a long say, which was translated by Gary Flanagan.

West of Da Nang.

Western Da Nang province, contingency recovery negotiations in a maintenance shed. Far left corner, Dr. Pete Miller; front right corner, the local military commander; beside him is Gary Flanagan. Across from him are the local village bosses. *Courtesy Buddy Newell*

At that table emerged the personal style I chose to do business with the local Vietnamese officials. In general, Vietnamese leaders are very consensus oriented: They want all of the involved parties to buy into a concept. I believe this may be more of a defense mechanism adopted for political survival in a one-party state (i.e., everyone shares the blame if things go south) rather than a generosity of spirit that values each party's ideas. At any rate, my working mantra was simple: Rather than tell them what we were going to do and how we were going to do it, I explained to them our objective and asked whether they could suggest a plan that would enable us to achieve it. In almost every case the course of action the Vietnamese proposed was nearly

The Da Nang contingency dig under way, with plenty of local suggestions for getting the job done. *Courtesy Buddy Newell*

identical to the plans we had already developed. More important, it became their plan as well, so they had to take ownership and work to see that each part was executed.

In the end we all agreed on what needed to be done on this recovery mission. We did not sign any papers, memorandums, or declarations. In the best West Texas tradition we did it all on a handshake and our word. These were country folks.

The recovery operation itself was not very complicated. The bulldozer had kicked up a skull, some odd medical devices such as old syringes and pill bottles, and a scrap or two of paper that appeared to be part of a U.S. Air Force field manual. All of the material was charred. The ground around it was already cleared by the bulldozer.

We knew this had been near the site of a U.S. field hospital during the war. More than likely we were dealing with part of a dump site. Pete Miller took a quick look at the partial skull and said was probably female and Asian. He carefully bagged the skull to turn over to the Vietnamese forensic lab in Hanoi. An hour later the small two-by-two-meter unit was clean and the screen empty. We had dug to the sterile layer and found nothing more worth noting.

We wrote a brief recovery report that afternoon, and by late evening I was back at the detachment in Hanoi, sitting on my balcony with a Tiger Beer in hand and gazing out over Lake Tay Ho, wondering who the woman was and what had happened to her.

Chapter 4
MY HOMETOWN: HANOI

After two months of nonstop adventure, the pace eased enough for me to rest a little and take a closer look at Hanoi before the next mission cycle began.

For a few weeks I had the luxury of becoming an evening and weekend tourist. After carefully reading the guide books, I poked into the nooks and crannies of the city and visited Ho Chi Minh's tomb, Hoa Lo Prison—the POW "Hanoi Hilton"—beautiful pagodas, Buddhist temples, thriving markets, and quiet parks. I even wandered in the warren of shops in the Hang Gai, the old, traditional neighborhood above Hoan Kiem Lake. In Ho Chi Minh City, anyone from Hanoi is considered a huckleberry from the back side of the mountains, which is probably why I felt at home with the country people in the very heart of the workers' paradise: the Socialist Republic of Vietnam.

As I mentioned before, in Saigon I had the same feeling as in LA; the pace was fast and furious, and the traffic was a nightmare. At least in Hanoi, if you get hit by a cyclo (a cycle rickshaw), it was just an accident. It's also no challenge to shop in Saigon because they have everything. In Hanoi shopping is fun because, to find what you want, say an American-sized coffee cup instead of a thimble, you have to look all afternoon and go into dozens of shops and back alleys. Of course, you're not going to find one anyway, but you go on an adventure. In Saigon I wouldn't dream of wandering around alone in the back streets without two or three mean friends, but, in Hanoi, *không sao!*—no big deal!—unless you happen to run into a soldier with an AK-47, which would be a government place not for curious "round eyes."

Ho Chi Minh's tomb, Hanoi.

Tran Quoc Pagoda, Tay Ho Lake, Hanoi.

Tran Quoc Pagoda, Hanoi.

The 140 Buddhas of Tran Quoc Pagoda tower, Hanoi.

In Saigon everyone had tipping down pat, an idea almost entirely foreign in Hanoi, except employees at the Hilton and cab drivers. When I tipped a barber ten thousand *dong* (sixty cents) after a two-dollar haircut, she came running after me saying I had forgotten my change. I always went to the local Communist barbershop, Cat Toc Nam (Lift Hair Men), a good place with no funny stuff like in those Saigon "babe-er shops" with their happy endings. In Hanoi people don't chat in barbershops, especially ones run by the Communist Party.

I started a photo collection, things I had seen on motorbikes, cyclos, and scooters. A family of four on a little 125cc moped was routine. Buddy claimed he saw a guy in a bathtub on a scooter; the guy was hugging the driver to keep the bike from upending. The principal means of transportation was motorbikes, bicycles, and cyclos; real motorcycles over 250cc were illegal. The few cars and trucks drove right in the middle of the road; that is, they split the white stripe even when coming from opposite directions; the motorbikes had all the rest.

In Vietnam we flew on Vietnam Air, we flew on Russian helicopters, we went into the mountains, we went into the swamps and jungles, but the most dangerous thing we did was cross a busy street. You just stepped out into the traffic, eyes straight ahead and keeping an exact speed while a river of motorbikes flowed around you. If you hesitated, chickened out, or stopped,

Hanoi, Ba Trieu Street.

you wrecked everybody's time-distance calculations and could cause a massive pileup. The second most dangerous thing was to ride in a vehicle on any road whatsoever. The Vietnamese had not adopted the concept of the seatbelt, of right of way, or of risk mitigation. I had yet to see a stop sign. The best solution while in a vehicle is to find interesting things to note left and right—looking ahead only generated a feeling of dread and terror. Somehow the Vietnamese developed a fairly efficient system to avoid head-on collisions, but it was so Asian and subtle, complete with driver body language, eye contact, headshakes, hand and arm signals that it remained one of those profound enigmas like the dreamtime or songlines of Aboriginal Australians, which are too obscure and mysterious to fathom, so I just trusted in the Lord.

My "hometown," Hanoi, was wonderfully friendly. One day I was walking in our neighborhood, Xuan Dieu Street (Zwan Zill), when a parade of Vietnamese junior-high kids on bicycles passed by, the first one giving me a high five, which meant I had to give twenty in a row. This is why one must always carry plenty of antibacterial wipes.

Our guards, drivers, maids, cook, and workers had a tendency to touch me or grab my hand, which showed respect to the *ông* (in Spanish, *jefe* or *padron),* but they would never touch the head, for they believed that would bring bad luck. On the Texas border, however, you should not admire a Hispanic baby *without* touching it on the head because that will bring bad luck. In Hanoi, if you inadvertently touch a baby's head, you must quickly tap both its shoulders to undo the curse.

So why was Hanoi my "hometown"? There were French buildings and marvelous, shaded boulevards, and the people moved as if they had all day. There were also lots of motorbikes, which honked their horns every five seconds. When drivers in Europe honk, it's to announce their importance and to tell you to get out of the way. In Hanoi, however, honking is more of a warning that you might get injured if you don't pay attention. Everyone smiles at you, and if you speak to them, they beam. The waiters, helpers, and shop staff were invariably cheerful, polite, and very disappointed if you gave the slightest indication of unhappiness. In Hanoi, unhappiness is a bad thing. I actually saw a no-smoking sign, which was in the conference room at the U.S. Embassy. I am pretty sure it was the only one in Hanoi—another concept that has not quite caught on.

Although it was the land of the "almost right," I admired the Vietnamese people for their incredible industry, day and night, Sunday to Sunday, when they were building, sawing, and hammering away; there was always the sound of things going up. We sometimes called it the "land of the almost right" because we were stuck with the Western idea of analyzing consequences and making detailed plans. As an example, a couple of days after I returned from the south, I complained about the condition of the stair railing in our new building; it was chipped, broken in a couple of places, and needed painting. I returned from an embassy meeting to find a beautiful, black-lacquer stair railing installed. However, the entire staff had to evacuate the building and go home to avoid being poisoned by the spray paint fumes. As a good take-charge infantryman I collected all of our fans, opened the doors and windows, and spent a good while introducing the painter to the idea of safety ventilation. The next week, when the painters painted the stairwell walls and scraped all of the spilt black-lacquer paint off our marble stairsteps, we introduced the concept of the drop cloth and masking tape to protect the marble stairs and the beautiful new black-lacquer railing. Bless them every one.

People in Hanoi often asked why I was there. By my clothes they knew I was not *tay ba lo* (round-eyed, backpacker youth who has only shorts and a T-shirt and spends no money). I just replied, Văn Phòng Mia-Hoa Kỳ (U.S. MIA Office). Almost everyone in Vietnam knew about us. I usually got a reaction of very polite but curious deference, but not the kind given to a big shot, more as one would treat a strange monk from a distant land, someone who had something to do with bringing back the dead. I think they found the whole idea a sort of vague Zen mystery, something not quite comprehensible. I did not exactly understand why this was so, but it was.

One evening Miss Tam, the cook, experimented again with American food. We had a tuna fish and mango sandwich deluxe. This is true. I ate it with a smile—mmmmm good! If she thought I was unhappy, she had a tendency to cry, which then made the Vietnamese staff wonder why I had been mean to her.

I had gotten a special invitation to attend the grand opening of the Metro, which is a German-type Wal-Mart, the first of its kind in Hanoi. The Metro carried half of the stuff I had shipped over. I got the special invitation because the store manager hoped he could supply the detachment with some of the tons of supplies we routinely fly over from Hawaii for each mission because they are unobtainable in country. There were five long speeches before the drums and dancing girls appeared. I went because I wanted to see how to run a very important public event in Hanoi; the deputy prime minister and a half-dozen other ministers were also there. The only thing that surprised me was that they were serving Tiger Beer at 7:30 AM, and all of the Vietnamese were being polite and naturally had their share. I kindly declined because Det 2 had an iron-clad rule that there was to be no drinking of any kind during the workday—no excuses. The Vietnamese, Australians, Brits, and Russians all thought our rule was bizarre.

Being the detachment commander had gotten a little lonely. In addition, since I was the boss, I could not allow myself to become close friends with any of the members of the detachment, besides the fact that they were almost all much younger than I. So I greatly enjoyed the arrival of the S3 operations officer, Lt. Col. Jay George, and his wife, Kysa, who both came to Hanoi for a few days. I took some time off to go around with them and help Kysa spend money in the wonderful shops I had discovered. It was a great boost to my morale to have a couple of casual friends again.

Part of my embassy country team life in Hanoi involved giving formal briefings on our mission to visiting dignitaries, congressional delegations, and foreign delegations, as well as participating in a host of media interviews. I was once interviewed for a Korean television station by a reporter who did not speak English. The official Vietnamese government translator did not speak Korean but did speak Japanese, as did the reporter. So my English words were first translated into Vietnamese, then Japanese, and then were eventually dubbed over in Korean, so to this day I have no idea what words were put into my mouth. The topic was a very sensitive one in that the reporter was developing a story on why the Korean government did not have an MIA program like the Americans did inasmuch as Korea had many MIAs from the Korean Army units that had fought on the side of the United States during the Vietnam War.

In the course of my part-time duties at the embassy I had gotten to know the attaché to the U.S. Department of Defense, Col. Steve Ball, and his wonderful wife, Allaine. Steve and Allaine had a beautiful house in Tay Ho district and were generous hosts on many important occasions such as Thanksgiving. One Sunday they invited me to go to church with them. Church was in a marvelous old colonial hotel, and the Protestant service was conducted by a Catholic priest, Father Charlie, who was assisted by a Vietnamese Baptist and an Australian Lutheran. Somehow it seemed perfectly normal for Hanoi, although it felt strange to put Vietnamese *dong* into the collection plate.

The new detachment consisted of a five-story and a seven-story building side by side. We used the five-story building for a conference room and for sleeping quarters for members of JTF-FA from Hawaii who were in country for more than a few days helping at the detachment. The seven-story building had our kitchen and dining room in the basement, a first-floor reception area complete with a large indoor fish pond, second-floor offices, and our apartments.

My balcony at the new Det 2 House on Xuan Dieu Street, Tay Ho district, after our move from the Ranch.

The new Det 2 House on Xuan Dieu Street.

To run these buildings required a considerable number of Vietnamese guards, a half-dozen house girls and laundry workers, a cook, and a couple of maintenance men. For a while the house staff was run by Miss Hoa, a very good-looking Vietnamese in her late twenties with a decent command of English. To distinguish her from our efficient, no-nonsense, extremely capable administrative assistant, Mrs. Hoa, the Det lads nicknamed her "Hottie" Hoa.

The house girls and ladies, particularly the head laundry worker, Miss My, did not get on well with Miss Hoa as they considered her something of a tart, as well as a tyrant. We were to have a big event at the detachment one Monday, so the Saturday before, Miss Hoa abruptly made all of the girls come in to clean. Normally we had only the bare minimum house staff on the weekends. About noon on Saturday Miss Hoa decided the girls had not cleaned well enough and announced they would have to work on Sunday as well, which, of course, made the girls furious and left many in tears. When I found out, I took Miss Hoa aside in private and explained that my God gets very angry if I make someone work on Sunday.

This shook her up a little, and she went away. A short time later she returned, saying she very often works on Sunday, and she knew I almost always did, so why should this God be mad? She was very clever. I told her I made special prayers and burned joss so that she, our guards, and I could work on

Sundays and that God said it was okay just for us but not for anybody else. She went away again with that look. To save face at the end of Saturday, she announced that, although she was completely dissatisfied with how filthy the place still was because the staff was too lazy to do a proper cleaning, the *ông*—over her objections—had decided it was clean enough for all of the important guests arriving Monday, and she would simply face Monday with her shame.

Almost all of our maids and cleaning girls were very young, cute, single, and hard working, and most of my guys were young, single, and hard working, and I had to constantly remind everyone that the government on both sides had a very specific clause in our formal treaty that absolutely forbade personal relationships between our two sides. Everyone would nod in pure innocence: Sure, sir, we all know that! I could not help but think that what they were actually saying was—but you are an old married guy, and we are pretty sure you don't see too well anymore, and we know you can't hear a damn thing except when you yell at us to turn the blankety-blank music down, and you aren't too nosy because all you do is work in your office on that big fat pile of papers or sleep in your apartment or fool around arranging rocks in the fountain in the lobby; your TV was off for a week, and you didn't even know it until one of the girls found out because she wanted to watch her soap opera while cleaning your place.

I had thought I would have a nice quiet life with my own kids grown and gone, but suddenly in Hanoi I again had six American and about as many Vietnamese kids to look after. Sometimes I felt like I was trapped in one of those MTV reality shows.

One day in November 2003 we had braced for a typhoon that failed to appear. The next afternoon, a perfect, sunny day, about midafternoon we watched the storm suddenly roll in from the west, where it had hidden in the mountains. A wall of wind-driven rain came across Tay Ho Lake and slammed into our building, shattering the glass doors to our rooftop and driving water though every window seal in the building. The entire Vietnamese staff and the detachment dived into action trying to shore up all the cracks and floods.

In the middle of all this chaos, Miss My, the chief laundry worker, sent up to Miss Hoa, the building boss, who went to Mrs. Hoa, the administrative assistant, who went to Sergeant Philip Revell, our operations NCO, who

Hanoi sunset over Tay Ho district after a typhoon.

went to Major Tom Dicken, the executive officer, and relayed the information that the colonel's shirt had a button that had taken a mind to suddenly leap off and that she would go out in the storm to find a needle and thread. I sent back down, *Không sao!* —no problem, I had a needle and thread. The passive voice in Asia is important because inanimate things do just decide to do such things; that way no one is to blame. Later I found the shirt on my bed with the button beside it. I put my trusty army sewing kit there and returned after supper to find that the button fairy had come to sew the pesky thing back on.

We had victory over the storm, which sent cracking lighting bolts crashing all around us, but the whole thing blew over in two hours, bringing the most incredible sunset, as if the entire sky was afire. Tom Dicken and I agreed that, of all the sundowns we had seen growing up in the West, none could compare to the one that evening over Hanoi.

Marine Corps Major Tom Dicken, from Oklahoma, was second in command of the detachment and on his second year in Hanoi. He was probably the most eligible bachelor in all of Hanoi, had a wide circle of friends, and was on everyone's A-list for social invitations. Of average height, he had a linebacker's build and in fact played on the local rugby team. Rugby was the in sport among the young Westerners in Hanoi. When England played Australia for the World Cup, the Hilton set up big screens, and nearly five hundred expats showed up for what was essentially a three-day beer party.

Every day near noon Tom would go down to the laundry room to have lunch with the house girls who were teaching him to speak Vietnamese. They took great delight in teaching him the wrong words for things, the substitute phrases usually having something to do with sex. Tom learned to check his newfound vocabulary with Buddy before using it in public. Tom was a generous soul with all he knew, round eye and Vietnamese alike. When he auditioned and earned a part in the choir for a visiting symphony's performance of *Carmina Burana* at the Hanoi Opera House, he got tickets for all of the ladies. Dressed in their finest, they sat together and cheered for him; they were so excited they chattered like little birds throughout the performance. When they turned around and waved up to my box, I would glare at them and warn them to be quiet, which settled them for perhaps five minutes.

One day as I was coming from the airport, we rolled up to the Det house to witness high drama on Xaun Dieu (Zwan Zill) Street. We arrived just in time to see the fat blonde German who lived two doors down come out of his gate on a motorbike and deliberately run over the mangoes that a street vendor was selling in front his place. She blasted him in the back of the head with a mango as he sped away, so he turned around, came back, and ran over the basket again.

Outraged, I grabbed the door handle to give him a little love nudge with a hundred pounds of SUV door when he went by. Buddy put his hand on me and suggested we sit still as the situation was going to get even uglier very quickly. I had learned to listen to Buddy. The street vendor blasted the German again, mango in the face this time; we cheered. He drove off, came back, and went into his house. By this time most of Xaun Dieu Street was milling about in front of his fence; the very large, angry crowd included our guards, whom I had to order back to work guarding us.

The street vendor and her sister both had long sharp knives, which they used to cut up the mangoes. They were waiting outside to carve up the German. Thankfully, a People's Committee official and the police arrived on motorbikes, and a long, long street court session ensued. The German came out of his house with his Vietnamese girlfriend, and the two of them hovered behind their locked gate while the trial progressed. They peered through the steel bars, and the German stuck his hands out now and then to gesture, which caused the mango ladies to slash in hopes of slicing off his fingers.

In the end everybody went away, and no fault was declared, but the German was too rude to pay for the mangoes, standing on the principle that it was illegal for the women to sell fruit on the street in front of his house. So, with the whole neighborhood against him, from then on something seemed to go wrong for him every time he turned around until he finally moved away. Funny how some people just don't get it.

I spent much of my spare time in Hanoi studying all I could find on Vietnam's fifty-four ethnic minority tribes because I realized very early on that they composed most of our field labor force. Pure Vietnamese live mostly on the coastal plain and in the broad river basins, while the minority tribes live in the hinterlands and mountains, where most of our recovery operations were conducted.

I needed to gain a basic understanding of tribal customs, taboos, social mores, religious holidays, superstitions, and especially dress so I could tell a Black Thai from a Red Dao, a H'mong from a Mon-Khmer. In addition to a few good bookstores that offered a couple of books on the subject, Hanoi had an excellent Museum of Ethnology covering most of the traditional tribal dress and daily life, as well as outdoor displays of the many types of architectural features and construction types used by various groups to build their distinctive village buildings.

I learned two things immediately, the first from reading, the second from watching. First, there is no such tribe or minority as "Montagnards," which was a French colonial appellation meaning "mountain person." Second, the pure Vietnamese of the lowlands are prejudiced against the ethnic minority tribes. While I was there, the government undertook a deliberate and well-publicized campaign to raise the minority tribes' standard of living and to improve their schools and public works, but the fact remains that the general Vietnamese population treats them as second-class citizens.

Chapter 5
POLITICS

IN MID-AUGUST 2003 it was time to start the cycle of negotiations that would lead up to the next thirty-day joint field activity and series of recovery operations. The typical cycle began with a back-and-forth between the operations and intelligence shops at JTF-FA headquarters in Hawaii, who were developing a list of primary and alternate recovery and investigative sites, and me, the detachment commander in Hanoi. Once we had settled on a basic list we would informally float it over to the VNOSMP office for a series of backchannel meetings, where we came to a basic agreement over what was feasible and what was not. Sometimes the sites would be in or near areas that had military restrictions. Usually we would strike them off but often would leave one or two on our list so that the VNOSMP would have to formally say no at the technical talks.

The technical talks were official meetings between the highest levels on each side and included the U.S. ambassador, the commanding general of JTF-FA, and the Vietnamese deputy minister of foreign affairs, who was also the head of the VNOSMP. The purpose of these discussions was to formally agree on which cases we would do next. They usually took place in Hanoi and included suits, speeches, statements, and signed diplomatic documents.

Shortly after the tech talks we would hold a large provincial coordination meeting, or "prov coord," down toward central Vietnam with the key players from each province and district where we were to work, all gathered in one place, and I, as chief of the U.S. MIA Office, would serve as the senior American. Every now and then at the prov coords we would hit a snag over a site if the VNOSMP had not done its homework or if something suddenly

Technical talks in Hanoi; Americans on the right, all with ties (too hot for jackets).

A provincial coordination meeting, Vinh, Nghe An province. Americans on the right, all in shirt sleeves. *Courtesy Buddy Newell*

changed, such as unannounced military maneuvers in an area. While official, these were much less formal affairs—nuts and bolts, open collar—that were followed by a big friendly dinner with plenty of beer and *cuoc lui* (pronounced kook low-ee), the fiery Vietnamese moonshine.

After the prov coords came weeks of preparation by the detachment for the fieldwork. Buddy Newell, our linguist, and I traveled all over the country doing site reconnaissance, visiting and evaluating the safety conditions of each selected case, verifying the feasibility of working, checking the availability of local labor, deciding on team living arrangements, and authorizing any advance work such as getting bamboo bridges built over streams, clearing jungle for the sites and helicopter landing zones, and cutting necessary trails.

Jungle hike, Quang Nam province.

Because all of this took place before we were able to start improving site access by ground or air, our work often entailed very long, tough jungle hikes.

It also involved a good deal of haggling with the VNOSMP over the cost of things. While growing up on the Rio Grande, in grade school I learned to bargain in the border markets and enjoyed it immensely. However, I made a political decision early on not to get involved in arguing with Vietnamese officials over money. Human nature being what it is, these arguments can get very emotional and hidden resentment can linger, which was contrary to my intent never to show anger to them, only deep, sad, profound disappointment if I didn't get my way. So, to his delight, I let Daniel do all the arguing.

Daniel Young, a Virginia expat in his midthirties, sported a shaved head and an earring, spoke fluent Vietnamese, and was a bit of a legendary character around Hanoi. I think he originally came to Asia with the UN but was now our brilliant logistics officer. He seemed to know everyone, where everything was, and how much it was really worth to the Vietnamese. His negotiations revolved around a great deal of shouting in Vietnamese, arm waving, slapping himself on the head, pounding his fist, turning his back and walking away, reluctantly being led back to the table by his arm, and a great beaming smile when he got his price, whether he was buying a few *dong*'s worth of bamboo poles or ten thousand cases of water. He often spent the weeks of mission preparation dashing madly between Hanoi, Hue, Da Nang,

Dong Ha, Ho Chi Minh City (Saigon), and elsewhere leasing warehouses, arranging supply trucks, buying barrels of machetes and other tools, making arrangements with airport customs, and doing the myriad of logistics chores associated with supporting teams spread across a thousand kilometers of Vietnam.

Meanwhile, our operations officer, Sergeant Philip Revell, and later Master Sergeant Mike Parks, both highly skilled USAF NCOs, were busy developing the concept of operations. The operations order would spell out in great detail where and when the teams would arrive in country, their movements to the site, how they would operate and close out, and their return to Hawaii. Of critical importance was the juggling of locations and flights of the four Russian helicopters we had contracted to support our operations. Both Philip and Mike were masters of the very efficient use of these air assets, and since we were charged by the flight hour, their mastery saved the American taxpayers a great deal of expense. Each detail of Philip's and Mike's operational plan had to be completely synchronized with Daniel's concept of logistics support or the whole thing would unravel. It was my job to put the entire plan under a microscope and find the flaws. However, since these warriors all knew their business, it was a rare occasion for me to find a disconnect.

After we did a final review within the detachment I would approve the operations order and send it to the team leaders in Hawaii, ideally a couple of weeks before they flew into country. When the teams arrived, we conducted a formal operations order with the entire group, usually in Da Nang because of its central location, so that all of the team members understood how they fit into the larger picture and what all the other teams were doing.

Typically woven into this cycle of preparing for the teams' arrival for a joint field activity were a number of political issues to be addressed, some serious, but most were only minor irritants. Shortly after I arrived in country, I set my sights on tackling a significant one: the issue of the restricted provinces.

In early 2003 the Vietnamese declared the provinces of Gia Lai, Kon Tum, Dac Lac, and what would become Dac Nong "restricted," meaning that JTF-FA operations could not be conducted in those areas. These were the provinces composing the Western Highlands on the border of southeastern Laos and east-central Cambodia, provinces containing the cities of Dak To, Kon Tum, Pleiku, An Khe, and Buon Ma Thuot. The Vietnamese authorities explained that the restriction was necessary because these areas had become dangerous, and they could not guarantee the teams' safety.

These areas had been a hotbed of resistance, particularly among the hill tribes that had worked with the Americans during the war. In the past few years they had also become a center of controversy over religious freedom, particularly H'mong Catholics and Baptists. American evangelicals, who infiltrated as tourists, had been handing out Bibles, setting up home churches, and, according to the Vietnamese government, inciting revolt against Hanoi. For a while the region had been off limits to all foreigners, but not long after I arrived, I began questioning tourists and discovered one or two that had recently gone to Pleiku with no problem.

Although I did not know the truth at the time, some weeks later I found out, when a Vietnamese official trusted me enough to explain what was behind our denied access to the restricted provinces. It turned out that a H'mong revolt had taken place in 2001, in which several government officials and policemen were murdered and four hundred of the defiant H'mong had escaped into Cambodia to a refugee camp. The Vietnamese had demanded that those responsible for the deaths be returned to face justice. Instead, the U.S. State Department in Washington, D.C. (not the U.S. Embassy in Hanoi) had granted visas to all of those H'mong and allowed them to enter the United States. When I was told this, it occurred to me that it would be like a Native American tribe doing the same thing, escaping to Canada, and then getting visas for France.

At the time, knowing only that the provinces were restricted but not exactly why, I decided to develop a political plan to get us back there so that we could work. It was a simple idea based on the army training methodology of "crawl, walk, run"—that is, start small and gradually build. I developed five criteria for picking the right case to pursue; it would have to be just across the province border, be a low-visibility case, entail minimum activity, make only small footprint, and not require a base camp. With the help of Gary Flanagan, a fellow Texan and the longtime chief of casualty resolution at the detachment, we began examining the various cases in those provinces and eventually settled on four or five possibilities, all involving the smaller investigative team rather than a complete recovery team. At first I did not tell anyone what I was up to. If word got around about this idea and the

Vietnamese eventually turned it down, the crowd of political grandstanders and MIA fringe straphangers could use the refusal as another example of how the Vietnamese were not cooperating with our effort. Vietnamese cooperation on the MIA issue was a political hot button and one about which every reporter and politician I met asked me.

The fact is they were cooperating well, with good reason. With the emergence of *doi moi,* or new economy, they wanted to join the World Trade Organization, and we were their sponsor. They also wanted access to our markets as they began decentralizing economic control and seeking direct investment from abroad, with provinces actually competing with each other for industry rather than having the location dictated by Hanoi. We wanted to resolve the MIA issue by trying to account for every MIA, and the Vietnamese seemed to have decided it was in their best interest to try to get this behind them. Although it was unspoken, both sides knew we had not only a mutual interest but also a shared threat in a certain neighboring Asian colossus. This was all soft power at work.

I watched *doi moi* unfold over the fall of 2003 and the winter of 2004. The new economy and direct foreign investment depended on e-commerce. When I first came to Vietnam, Internet cafes were primitive 56-baud affairs nearly exclusively for Westerners. By the time I left, in the summer of 2004 there were high-speed DSL operations in the post office of almost every major city in the country, and they were available to anyone who walked in and put their *dong* down. The scope and speed of this development were breathtaking.

I created a short briefing on the plan for getting a toehold in the restricted provinces and shared it with a select few at headquarters—Brig. Gen. Redmann and old-timers Joel Patterson and Dickie Hites, as well as the new J3 operations officer, Lt. Col. Dave Buckingham. We agreed it was worth pursuing and selected the case that best met the criteria. Joel warned, however, that if we brought this case up at the formal tech talks right now, the Vietnamese would be forced to say no as apparently someone above the VNOSMP was setting the restrictions. We decided that it would be best for me to go offline with Mr. Dao, ask to do this easy case, and have him try to persuade his superiors that officials in Washington, D.C., saw the restrictions as an example of Vietnamese noncooperation in the MIA issue.

Mr. Dao and his staff at VNOSMP seemed startled when I showed up alone at their office for our meeting to iron out the last details of the upcoming mission cycle. Buddy was on leave in the States, and Gary Flanagan was escorting some VIP, so I had no interpreter to take with me. Normally this would result in having to reschedule, but I got the bright idea that it was another chance to make them think I might be just a little unpredictable. Giang kept looking past me to the door, waiting for someone to follow. Pham Trong Giang was Mr. Dao's very hip young assistant and was also a friend of Buddy's. Not until I casually sat down in a comfortable chair next to Mr. Dao and accepted his offer of green tea did they realize that I had indeed come alone, that I had no American witness to the conversation, and furthermore that I did not seem to care. This was something nearly incomprehensible in their world of political self-preservation.

Then Mr. Dao leaned toward me, very close; I thought he was going to take my hand to hold, which is not unusual in Vietnam, but I knew he was too worldly to do so. In a quiet voice he started talking about the House amendment to the State Department authorization bill on human rights in Vietnam. He said that it made the people of Vietnam angry and that it was now difficult to secure necessary permissions from the very top of the government. I replied that in the United States the government can't tell congresspersons what to do but that not all Americans agreed with the resolution. Besides, I added, I was just a simple soldier and did not have anything to do with the politics of it; I suggested that he discuss it with the political counselor and added that there was no connection between our humanitarian mission and that issue. He replied that he had just wanted to make sure once again that we knew he was upset and that the resolution made difficulties for all of us.

I brought out my atlas, and we went over the basic locations of the upcoming seventy-fifth joint field activity. I then switched to Spanish and began discussing the importance of case number such and such and how we needed to get the investigative team in there. It took him a few minutes to realize I was pointing just east of An Khe—in one of the restricted provinces. I pointed out that this case was only a few kilometers across the Gia Lai border, that the investigative team could be in and out of there in only a day or so, and that we knew that tourists went to An Khe, so it could not be dangerous.

In addition, it would show real progress if we could do it in this JFA, but we wanted to discuss it with him before we put it on the list. Careful not to overreact, he said to give him a chance to think about it and in Spanish said there should be a private discussion on the matter later.

A few days later I met a high Vietnamese official alone for lunch in an upscale Western restaurant. After pleasantries, I explained that we were under a great deal of pressure to show progress during the next joint field activity, not later. I added that it would be most appropriate if the Vietnamese could demonstrate this progress as Brig. Gen. Redmann, a true friend of Vietnam, was leaving command of JTF-FA. I explained that I had to brief eleven congressmen the next day and said that they were going to ask me whether we were making progress with regard to the restricted provinces (they did not ask).

We discussed a number of case options, none promising, but he finally latched on to a specific case, one I had already decided would be our fallback position after working it out with Ron Ward, the research and investigation team leader. It was a very simple, low-key concept. We agreed in principle that he, the Vietnamese official, would give his most considerate thought to letting me personally take one RIT guy directly to Pleiku, Gai Lai province, to conduct a very important interview with this seventy-seven-year-old witness, someone who was surely too old and weak to travel outside the province for an interview. Of course, neither of us knew whether the elderly witness could travel, and it did not matter; it was a plausible scenario. I said this would be progress.

The Vietnamese official indicated he would tell me the day before the tech talks began if he had persuaded his superiors to give permission. If so, we should quietly add the case number to the official list but under no circumstances mention the case or publicly discuss it during the tech talks; it would just be another case number on the final approved list.

He did not call me the day before the tech talks, so we could not put the case number on the list, but to me it was just a matter of going after it again next time; sooner or later we would get there, and we did. In 2005 the detachment once again began limited operations in the restricted provinces. The issue of the restricted provinces is but one example of the maze of political complexities and subtleties associated with the MIA mission. At the end of this maze, digging the sites was simply the most direct stage.

At the end of August 2003 we took off down Route 1 from Hanoi, 250 kilometers south to the city of Vinh in Nghe An province, to talk to several engineers about an upcoming mission. Everybody who heard we were going to Vinh just shook their head in sympathy because they knew that the country accent of the citizens of Nghe An is impossible for Americans to understand. In addition, the people are hard headed toward the central government because Ho Chi Minh was born in Vinh, which was also the birthplace of the Viet Minh revolution against the French. All in all the citizens there don't take guff from anybody. They don't like being told what to do, and they don't like foreigners of any kind. As a Texan, I pretty well related to that. During the American War, as they call it, Vinh was the southern terminus of the railroad that brought down supplies for the Ho Chi Minh Trail. It was a permanent secondary target for any pilot who could not bomb his primary target. We did our best to level the place.

For the first couple of hours south of Hanoi we wound through the dramatic limestone spires and mountain crags of the provinces of Nam Dinh, Ninh Binh, and Than Hoa, dodging bicycles, cattle, goats, pony carts, and the broken-down buses that make Route 1 a true motoring adventure. Finally, where Route 1 parallels the South China Sea down to Vinh, the high country gave way to the vast rice fields, Brahman cows, and water buffalo of Nghe An.

The city of Vinh was rebuilt by the East Germans in the 1970s and had all the charm of the dingiest parts of East Berlin when the wall was still up.

Route 1, Ninh Binh province.

Route 1, Than Hoa province.

However, a six-block maze of alleys forms the Vinh market, one of my favorites in the country. It was rare to see a round eye in Vinh, and the people were very interested and friendly. When asked where I was from, I always insisted Hanoi, which immediately produced that curious, charming way they cover their mouths when laughing.

Exploring the market I bought a fully flashing, electric-lighted, whirly round Buddha, kind of like one of those old beer clocks, which I thought would be just perfect for our bar at the detachment in Hanoi. When we returned to Hanoi, Buddy wouldn't let me hang it up, explaining it might be considered as an insult by the Buddhists on our staff.

We were in Vinh to have a preliminary meeting with the provincial and the city officials to start the planning for a very complicated future case, an aircraft crash site that was at the bottom of a large pond surrounded by houses and a new building. Our engineers were certain that, if we drained the pond, the foundations of the houses would collapse. This required a very complex engineering mitigation plan. The concept was to drive down into the border of the pond a huge steel box consisting of twelve-meter-deep interlocking plates. On the interior of the box would be an I-beam skeleton to support the walls. To complicate matters further, the city phone and power lines ran directly over the pond, so they would have to be rerouted. We intended to drain the pond with a giant marine pump we had brought from Hawaii and then to excavate with a suspended bucket loader and dump trucks.

Examining our blueprints and drawings, the Vinh officials were surprisingly confident that the concept would work. The more politically delicate issue was their insistence that we hire a Vietnamese company to execute the work, whereas we had intended to bring in an American, German, or Australian firm. In the end we decided to take a chance with the Vietnamese, in this case a Vietnamese army engineer battalion, thinly disguised as a private company since we did not have formal military-to-military relations with Vietnam. If something were to go seriously wrong, at least it would remain internal to the Vietnamese government.

At the end of the meeting I stated that I wanted to make one final but critical request. They poised with their pencils, prepared to write, as they had captured every word I had uttered during the entire meeting. Was it possible to go over to the park and take a picture with my driver, Mr. Thinh, and the world's largest statue of Uncle Ho Chi Minh? They cracked up, saying *vâng vâng* (okay, sure!). They were very proud that I understood how important this was. To be honest, I knew it was important to Mr. Thinh, and he grinned the entire ten hours back up Route 1 to Hanoi.

A week later we were back in Vinh for the provincial coordination meeting with the officials from all of the provinces where we intended to work. The deputy VNOSMP, Tran Van Tu, and I continued our back and forth on the cost of the complex site in Vinh. Although I had decided I would not get involved in negotiating over money, this was a big site and quite expensive. The Vietnamese were not used to negotiating with us before the work,

Vinh, Nghe An province; Mr. Thinh gets his picture taken with the world's tallest statue of Ho Chi Minh.

only after, thus knowing exactly the incurred cost rather than the estimate of future risk. We were both under pressure because we were running out of time, but after a few more meetings we came to a mutually satisfactory conclusion.

There were four unusual aspects of this provincial coordination meeting in Vinh. First, it was held before the high-level technical talks in Hanoi because the senior officials' schedules grant that Hanoi meeting until we were too close to the start of the mission. As a result, most of the sticky issues were worked out at the grass-roots level. Later the tech talks went well because of this, so both we and the Vietnamese began considering permanently reversing the order of the meetings.

Second, the Vietnamese gave permission for the Vinh site to start early and extend as necessary to complete the project, in this case almost two months beyond the standard thirty-day joint field activity. They had done the same thing on the last JFA for the site in Vung Tau. This soon became more routine for difficult sites.

Third, we had decided to add to the list the case number of the very important interview in Pleiku with the seventy-seven-year-old witness, the one who was surely too old and weak to travel outside the restricted province of Gai Lai. We did not discuss this either at Vinh or at the tech talks, and for the first time at either meeting we left out any mention of the restricted provinces. This indirect approach eventually brought a small victory. In July 2005, in conjunction with Vietnamese prime minister Phan Van Khai's visit to the United States the investigative team was allowed into the restricted province to conduct this interview in Pleiku.

While we were in the middle of discussions in Vinh, the Quang Tri province representative, Mr. Hoang Nam, approached Buddy and handed him a piece of paper, a dogtag rubbing he said came from a citizen, who also claimed to have found remains associated with the dogtag. Buddy didn't react at first because this sort of thing happened frequently and it rarely turns out to be anything useful; often it is part of a bone trade scheme. Sitting across the table, I watched Buddy on his laptop, punching in the name on Bright Light, our extensive database.

Suddenly his eyes widened a bit. With a slight smile he scribbled a note to me, "Case 1040, SFC Kenneth Hanna, Lang Vei Special Forces Camp,

Quang Tri Province." The last thing we wanted was for this to become public knowledge until we could get someone there to investigate. If it were true, the citizen who had the remains could easily be subject to bribes, might sell the remains, and could even be in danger as it was a commonly held belief among the less-educated Vietnamese that American remains were worth a fortune and a ticket to the United States, none of which was true.

We had a quiet conversation with Mr. Tu and Mr. Nam and agreed to add case 1040 to the list and send the investigative team there. We also agreed that Mr. Nam, from Quang Tri, would go back and consult the witness to try to verify the story. If it appeared true, we would not wait for the mission window but would launch an immediate contingency operation.

After ten hours on Route 1 racing back from Vinh, I had but a few minutes to dash upstairs and change into a suit and tie and report to a formal dinner with our Vietnamese helicopter company to sign next year's contract. Since we did not have an official military-to-military relationship with the country, the Vietnamese army aviation regiment was operating as a commercial contract helicopter company. Our pilots were very senior colonels who had flown for years in one of the most rotary-wing-hostile environments on the planet. I myself had flown in helicopters for decades and had a great deal of experience. Visitors would ask me whether I was comfortable flying with these senior pilots. I'd answer that it was always better to fly with an old Vietnamese pilot than a young American hotshot who thinks he is flying a Corvette.

The staff had told me I did not have to make a speech at the dinner. The government minister stood and gave a long talk and a toast. He was followed by the head of the helicopter corporation, who was then followed by the boss of the helicopter contract group that we actually flew with. When he sat down, all eyes turned to me. The room was full of Vietnamese army helicopter pilots wearing the blue company uniform. Our contract would feed their families for the next year.

I stood, raised my glass, and said that I was a simple soldier who had been flying with army helicopter pilots for thirty years. I said I could not tell any difference in the great skill of the Vietnamese and the American pilots. In addition, if I had the nerve to ask them to fly to some crazy place, they had the guts to try it, American or Vietnamese. Like any soldier, I was just glad, like them, to get a good meal and free beer at the expense of the big bosses. I closed with a toast to the extraordinary good looks and raw courage of helicopter pilots. Needless to say I had forty new best friends.

Buddy was leaning at my shoulder the entire evening, quietly translating. By this time I had learned to speak in short rhythmic phrases, making it easier and effective to translate. He was very attuned to this rhythm, knowing exactly when I would pause. I had also discovered that these pauses for his translation made me a better speaker because I could take advantage of the break to clearly form my next words.

Buddy and I spent countless hours together in many difficult situations, and I grew very fond of him and trusted him implicitly. By the year's end I had come to think of him as a dear friend and second son. He became not only translator and linguist but also protector, bodyguard, confidant, wise counselor, and sounding board. He had a wry sense of humor and wicked wit and at times was something of a prankster.

Hailing from Mobile, Alabama, William H. "Buddy" Newell III was thirty-seven years old, stood six feet tall, had broad stocky shoulders, a crewcut, glasses, and a ready smile. In the mid-1980s he enlisted in the air force at age nineteen, went to the Defense Language School, and then on to Okinawa, where he was a "dogger," a Vietnamese linguist for a military program that required such skills. Eventually that operation ended, and when Joint Task Force–Full Accounting was created in 1992, many of the old doggers came to it as linguists. When JTF-FA Detachment 2 set up shop in Hanoi, Buddy was one of the first handful of Americans back in Vietnam.

He eventually left the service but remained in Vietnam, where he spent five years in Saigon as a businessman before returning to the detachment as a civil service linguist. While in Saigon he met and married Diep, daughter of a former South Vietnamese army sergeant who had survived the reeducation camps. Buddy's daughter, Megan, attended grade school at the International School, along with the kids from most of the Western embassies.

Buddy's Vietnamese skills were unparalleled. Fluent in both the northern and southern dialects, he was a true scholar and spent hours studying a thick Vietnamese dictionary. I once heard him gently correct the Vietnamese of a high government minister by suggesting he had used the wrong word. With a light laugh, the minister acknowledged and adopted Buddy's correction.

When we traveled, one of my favorite things was go to a restaurant off the beaten path, where Buddy would order by pointing to the menu but not speak. Invariably the bored waitresses would gossip or joke about the two round eyes at the table. I enjoyed their startled surprise when eventually Buddy teased them in perfect Vietnamese.

We shared an appreciation of the absurd and a quirky sense of humor. For example, consider *phuo.* Pronounced "fhuh," *phuo* means flat rice noodles served in a bowl, the ubiquitous Vietnamese breakfast, a dish that can be properly made only in Hanoi. When we were in Hue, Da Nang, or somewhere down south, I would ask the waitress if the *phuo* was from Hanoi. No, was always the reply. Then it must be "faux *phuo,*" I'd say. Buddy and I cracked up while the poor girl eyed us like a couple of village idiots.

Chapter 6
CROSSING THE RIVER STYX

Why suffer'st thou thy sons, unburied yet,
To hover on the dreadful shore of Styx?
Make way to lay them by their brethren.

—William Shakespeare,
Titus Andronicus, Act 1, Scene 1

AT HIS BASE CAMP in Vietnam, JPAC anthropologist August Goodman used to post on his tent this quote by Titus Andronicus, the Roman general returning from the Gothic Wars, bearing his lost sons for burial in their homeland. In Greek mythology the River Styx was the underworld river separating the worlds of the living and the dead.

A few days after we returned from Vinh, Mr. Tu called and said the Quang Tri officials had arranged a meeting with two witness from Lang Vei, who now claimed to have two sets of remains to turn over. He said we had permission to do the contingency mission and that we should all go immediately. It was a mad scramble to pack, order plane tickets, make vehicle arrangements in Hue, and head to the airport. Fortunately, we had an anthro in country, Dr. Pete Miller, who had just arrived to familiarize himself with the giant pump we had brought in for his big dig in Vinh. He would drive south from Vinh and meet us in Dong Ha.

Buddy, Gary Flanagan, and I headed to the airport to fly to Hue and drive to Dong Ha, where we would meet Mr. Tu and our other VNOSMP counterparts before driving on to Lang Vei via Khe Sanh.

During the Tet Offensive of 1968, when the People's Army of Vietnam (PAVN) and the Viet Cong were laying siege to the Marine base at Khe Sanh, the Special Forces built a camp a few miles away at Lang Vei. The camp was well suited to observe the Lao border, which was a mile and a half away and was manned by twenty-four Green Berets and about nine hundred Bru and Ca tribesmen, who formed a mobile strike force. Near midnight on February 6, 1968, the camp came under attack by the PAVN 66th Regiment, supported by ten PT-76 light tanks. In a fight that lasted well into the next morning, the PAVN overran camp, killing ten Americans and wounding thirteen. Because it was the first time in the war that the PAVN used tanks against U.S. forces, Lang Vei became a legendary battle in Special Forces circles.

Although some of the Green Beret dead were recovered, we had five MIA from the site, as well as a missing A-1 Skyraider pilot who was shot down nearby while attacking the tanks. The name on the dogtag rubbing we had seen at Vinh, SFC Kenneth Hanna, was last seen with Master Sergeant Charles Wesley Lindewald Jr. The two were observed taking cover in a bunker on the southwest of side the camp just before one of the PAVN tanks lumbered up and fired into the bunker. The JTF-FA had done a number of recovery operations at the old camp in 1994–1995, but it was a very large site—two hills with perhaps fifty old caved-in bunkers—now a heavily vegetated banana plantation.

Landing in Hue, we met our driver and took off north up Route 1 to Dong Ha to spend the night in a no-star hotel. Dong Ha was the last town before the DMZ. The hotel was kind of interesting, an art-deco holdover from the French era, and I do mean authentic art deco, as in the original paint, curtains, and furniture. It had one English TV channel, Fashion TV, which broadcast a special on male models that night. We watched Vietnamese soap operas.

Early the next morning, following the van carrying Mr. Tu and Colonel Mao, we headed west on Route 9, just below the old DMZ, and into the Khe Sanh, the vast, sparsely settled mountains of western Quang Tri province, mostly occupied by H'mong and Chu-ru minorities. North of the town of Khe Sanh we stopped to wander around the plateau of the famous marine firebase, walk the old runway, and take pictures with Tiger Tooth Mountain in the background. Some of the old bunkers were still there, but one had to be cautious while exploring because unexploded ordnance still littered about such places.

Passing through the unmemorable little town of Khe Sanh, we pushed ten kilometers farther west, pulling up at the Lang Vei People's Committee Building, a surprisingly handsome two-story structure with a red tile roof, tall white columns, and wide upper and lower verandas freshly painted a pleasant beige.

Inside we had a friendly meet and greet with about twenty central government, province, district, village, and hamlet officials, including Mr. Man,

Into the terrain of the Khe Sanh, Quang Tri province.

The old U.S. Marine Corps airstrip at Khe Sanh firebase; Tiger Tooth Mountain in the background.

the local party secretary; Mr. Hien, the People's Committee deputy chairman; and Mr. Tuan, the police chief. Finally the two witnesses arrived—two young men dressed in their best tattered jeans and finest dirty T-shirts. They entered the room literally shaking in fear, repeatedly bowing their heads before taking a seat at the long conference table. I don't think they had ever been in a meeting in their lives and certainly had never been around so many officials. I whispered to Buddy to take their pictures since, if they disappeared on us, it might help us find them again. Buddy coolly moved to the head of the table and politely asked everyone to smile for the camera for what they all assumed was a group photo.

Lang Vei contingency recovery operation; meeting with officials and witnesses. Far left corner, Dr. Pete Miller; Gary Flanagan to my right. *Courtesy Buddy Newell*

Of course, every official had to make a short speech, but after a while we finally got the witnesses to tell their story. They were at Lang Vei hunting for metal, in this case probably trespassing on the banana plantation, and Buddy whispered to me that it was a wonder they were still alive since the place is full of unexploded ordnance. While metal hunting they noticed a hole in the ground, a collapsed bunker, and bones sticking out. They recovered the bones of two people, and each of them kept one set. Yes, they were willing to take us there, and, yes, they would give us the remains.

We piled into vehicles and drove a short distance to Lang Vei hill, just off Highway 9 to Lao. The witnesses led us to a four-foot hole in the ground, a collapsed bunker on the northeast corner of the hill. The original search area was based on reports from eyewitnesses to the battle, who had placed the two in a bunker on the southwest corner of the hill, probably two hundred meters away. There was a Vietnam-era combat boot and part of a poncho liner next to the bunker. Pete Miller, Gary Flanagan, and I began mapping and photographing the site while Buddy jumped down for a close examination of the bunker.

We finished our recording and then drove a short distance to Tan Hao hamlet in Tan Lien village, Huong Hoa district, where we took a long walk on a muddy trail to reach the house of the older witness. Much of the village crowded around us in the yard, where we sat in the broiling sun at a table with the family of the witnesses to discuss the next step. The older witness was married, and his wife and mother sat beside him at the table. He said quietly

Mapping the bunker at Lang Vei; Gary Flanagan on the right; Lao border, Route 9 in the background. *Courtesy Buddy Newell*

Near Lang Vei after negotiations in the yard of a witness.

that he suddenly had second thoughts about turning over the remains. We expected this because it meant, how much money will you give me?

I leaned over the table and spoke in a low voice to the older witness, while Buddy, understanding my true intended audience, translated just loudly enough for the gathered villagers to hear. It was a long speech about cooperation and mentioned that the issue was much larger than the hamlet or the village. It involved both of our nations moving forward together for the future, as well as the personal grief of the families of the two lost Americans. I spoke of the false, evil rumor in Vietnam that the U.S. government paid fortunes for remains, for that was not the truth. When I said it was not possible to give him money because my government does not allow sacred remains to be held hostage, the wife started crying, her dreams of a new house evaporating. They offered to give us a few bones for identification. Impossible, I said. It would be all or nothing because if we started that practice, the remains would wind up in the hands of bone traders, who would try to sell them one rib at a time, mostly to other misinformed Vietnamese. I made it clear that it was all or nothing and that if I left that day empty handed, they would not even have the labor compensation after the identification was made. In short, they would have nothing.

My Vietnamese counterparts, Mr. Tu and the Quang Tri province representative, Mr. Nam, explained that they could be fairly reimbursed for the labor they expended and receive storage compensation, which would be a fair amount. However, this would happen only after the remains had been identified, which meant they had to be turned over first to be sent to the lab. For several hours we used every argument we could muster while remaining very calm, almost casual in tone, which was important in this situation. We knew from the beginning that the old mother wanted her son to do the right thing, so we kept working on her. How would you feel, asked Mr. Tu, if we came and took the remains of your ancestors and held them for money? The old woman burst into tears. It was an intense scene, charged with a thick pathos for all.

I could tell the village police chief wanted to beat up both witnesses on the spot. It was also evident that the local judgment was rapidly turning against the witnesses. The locals were getting nervous because they were afraid that these officials were going to be mad at the village, meaning real trouble in the future. There was a lot of face at stake for the local government officials because the American officials had come all the way from Hanoi and were about to be embarrassed by failure.

The weird thing was that I was just sitting there at the table listening, almost ready to give up, trying to figure out my next move, when I thought—Hey, God, I could use a little help here, and I promise to go to church next Sunday. Out of the crowd pushed a middle-aged man, striding straight up to the table, shoving his finger in the face of the young witness, and ordering him around back of the house. It turned out older brother was taking kid brother to the woodshed. The youngster came back in about two minutes, said he would return immediately with the remains, and rushed off on his motorbike. This set off the mother of the other witness, and then he, too, finally rose and disappeared into his jungle hiding place. We held our breath.

Witnesses turning over remains from Lang Vei for measurement and detailed inventory; Dr. Miller is starting the layout process. The image is blocked in the photo out of respect for the families. *Courtesy Buddy Newell*

Each witness returned with bundles, two large, white rice sacks, but would not approach our laying out and inventory spot until they had placed burning joss sticks all around in a circle. Finally, each one came to the center of the joss ring, bowed, and meekly placed his bundle on the ground near Dr. Miller. Because of the significant amount of remains, the inventory took a while. Pressing against the yellow crime scene tape Pete Miller had thoughtfully brought along, the villagers watched us carry out the painstaking measuring and recording process.

Every veteran understands that bit of lingering guilt of surviving when others did not. We all deal with that in our own way, and mine had been not to dwell on it because there is no rhyme or reason. I sat cross-legged on the ground, surrounded by rising wisps of sweet incense smoke, a rice bag of bones in my lap, handing them one by one as precious treasure for Pete to lay out, measure, and record—a careful survey. As I studied each tibia, fibula, and metacarpal, my senses gradually transformed as slowly flooding water, rising into another universe, a surreal epiphany, my mind not right, Camus' existential abyss, peering over the deep chasm into eternal darkness, each chalky bone easily my own except for the blessing of the gods, fate, karma. My world turned again in that instant. It was a moment in time I shall struggle with until released among the heavens.

Finally we closed and sealed the metal Pelican cases and walked back down the muddy trail to the road.

This sort of remains turnover was rare, and it had been three years since the last one. We had three or four phone calls or walk-ins a month, but they were always either a scam or a dead end. Even Mr. Tu and Mr. Nam were astonished that we pulled off the recovery. Once we got back to the road where no one could observe us, we celebrated like little kids. I never in my life imagined I would have a bear hug with a Communist government official.

In the middle of the deserted road we leaned on the hood of a vehicle filling out the forms for the official handover to our counterparts for transport back to Hanoi. We had the remains of two Special Forces soldiers that folks have been looking for for thirty years. Of course, nothing could be announced until the CIL lab did the identification, but I had no doubt about who we had, the dental evidence alone was so good that even I could see the correlation to the record. This would be good news in the Special Forces community, and that circle was so tight that I knew the news would soon making the rounds as we had a considerable number of SF guys in JTF-FA. I did go to church the next Sunday.

As soon as the recovery teams arrived in country in October 2003 we sent one team to dig the bunker site to ensure we had recovered any and all bones that remained. The remains secured from the contingency recovery were those of Special Forces Sergeant First Class Kenneth Hanna from Scranton, South Carolina, and Master Sergeant Charles Wesley Lindewald Jr. from La Porte, Indiana. The CIL lab announced the identification of the remains on September 8, 2004. In January 2005 SFC Hanna was buried at Fayetteville, North Carolina, and MSG Lindewald was buried in Arlington National Cemetery in April 2005.

It was late afternoon by the time we had completed the paperwork with our Vietnamese counterparts. Returning to our vehicle, we told our driver, Mr. Thinh, that we knew he loved to sleep in Dong Ha, but if he was skilled enough, he could get us all the way to Hue by dark. We had a flat-out rule about not driving on the highways after dark unless you are absolutely intent on the complete destruction of a government vehicle, as well as suicide. I dare not describe the trip, but we arrived in beautiful Hue about a millisecond before the very last, honestly truthful instant of what could approximately be called daylightlike conditions. We went straight to the courtyard bar of the majestic French colonial Saigon Morin Hotel, my favorite hotel in Vietnam.

I had been through Hue several times but never had a chance to look around. The next morning we had a couple of hours before our plane back to

Hanoi, so Buddy and I hiked across the Truong Tien bridge on the Perfume River and went to the old Imperial City of Hue and the Citadel, which guards two imperial palaces. The front face of the Citadel, the Flag Tower, scene of one of the toughest Tet '68 battles of the war, is the most imposing military architecture I had ever seen. Even though it is very sobering, once you get inside it is a thing of true beauty. We explored Thai Hoa Palace and were making our way along a grassy trail to Truong Sanh Palace, when a golden cobra slithered across the path a few feet in front of us. I grew up in West Texas with rattlesnakes all around and was not afraid of snakes, but a cobra is not a rattlesnake. While Buddy chased the cobra to get a closer look, I did an aboutface back to Thai Hoa Palace to look at postcards of Truong Sanh Palace to see what I was going to see if I ever went there again. Although largely

The Citadel at Hue.

Thai Hoa Palace, Hue.

wrecked in the war, the Vietnamese government has done an excellent job of restoring the palaces and temples and preserving old Imperial Hue.

On September 30, 2003, I conducted my first repatriation or "repat" ceremony at Hanoi's Noi Bai Airport. This involved the formal honors and sendoff of any remains we had recovered. There was a similar ceremony in Hawaii when the plane arrived. Except for the annual U.S. Marine Corps ball and the embassy's Fourth of July bash hosting all of the other embassies, the repat is the only other time I was allowed to wear a military uniform.

This repat, like most, was conducted on the tarmac near the rear of the U.S. Air Force C-17 that had flown in the repat team, crisply uniformed members of all services detailed from the CIL lab and JTF-FA headquarters in Hawaii. The four sets of remains were encased in three-foot wooden boxes

Repatriation ceremony, Noi Bai Airport, Hanoi, September 2003.

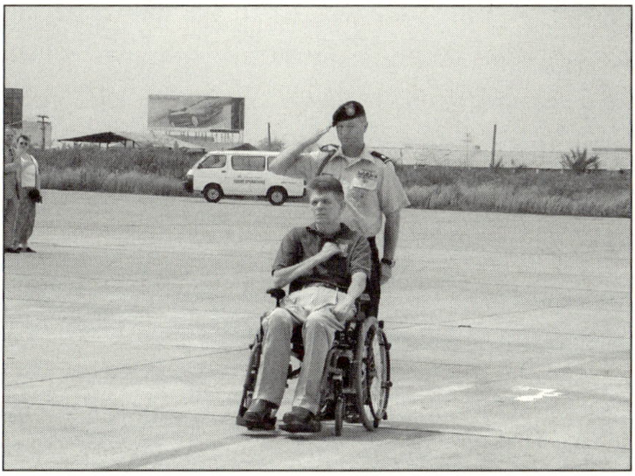

Tom Corey, president of the Vietnam Veterans of America, rendering final honors; repatriation ceremony, Noi Bai Airport, Hanoi, September 2003.

Formal loading of the transfer cases, repatriation ceremony, Noi Bai Airport, Hanoi, September 2003. The civilian crowd always included local Australians, New Zealanders, and British.

on a table. After a careful mutual inventory, Mr. Tu and I signed paperwork at the table, sealing the top of each box with screws.

Off to one side gathered a large crowd, most of the Americans, Brits, and Aussies living in country, as well as a scattering of other Westerners and a handful of reporters. Since the ambassador was traveling, Ray Porter, deputy chief of mission, stood beside me. Our special guest of honor, in his wheelchair on my left, was Tom Cory, president of the Vietnam Veterans of America. It was a silent ceremony, which was a good thing because there always seemed to be a very loud Vietnamese aircraft testing its jet engines next to the repat anytime we did it in Hanoi.

The uniformed detail marched down the ramp of the aircraft and halted with a salute before me. One by one the wooden boxes were solemnly carried to flag-draped aluminum transfer cases and sealed inside. I pushed Tom Cory's wheelchair, following the last transfer case. When we halted at the ramp, Tom and I rendered a long, final salute to our fallen comrades before the aircraft roared off westward toward Hawaii. As we watched it disappear over the horizon, I was thinking that, in all my long career, I had never felt such a powerful sense of accomplishment and profound satisfaction. I was completely humbled by the honor to command this mission.

Chapter 7
VIENTIANE AND PHNOM PENH

I HAD TO FLY TO LAOS for a few days to do some business with Johnny Strain, the affable Special Forces lieutenant colonel who commanded Detachment 3 in Vientiane, the capital of Laos. Since we were not supposed to fly Lao Air, I had Mrs. Hoa specifically book a ticket on Vietnam Air. I asked the counter agent whether the flight was Vietnam Air, and, of course, it was, just as the ticket said. When I got to the bottom of the ramp, I could see the blue tail with the champa flower and leaf logo of Lao Air, not the white tail and golden lotus blossom I was expecting. It was, however, a new Airbus, which appeared to be in good condition, and the pilots were either Australians or New Zealanders. Since the flight took only an hour or so, it was daylight, the weather was good, and there were no more flights that day, I boarded—and hoped for the best.

Over the rugged, unexpectedly high mountains of western Laos I drank my green tea while taking in the remoteness below. Although Laos is a one-party Communist state, at the airport the authorities seemed rather uninterested in the arrival of foreigners. I was met by Johnny Strain's Lao driver, who, palms together, greeted me with a bow and a gentle "Sabbai dee," and whisked me pasted his customs buddy, who stamped my diplomatic passport and issued a visa on the spot.

I was still in baggage claim when my cell phone rang; the caller was a radio reporter from Washington, D.C., who wanted an interview about the MIA mission. Since the Public Affairs Office at headquarters had not given me a heads-up, I knew she had bypassed the entire Department of Defense media chain. She had gotten my number from an AP reporter friend of mine in Hanoi. It was three AM in Washington, D.C., so I said if she was crazy enough to stay up all night to get an interview, and since I had never done a radio interview from a cell phone in Laos, it would be just dandy to chat with her. We talked as I rode through the city.

Vientiane did not seem like much of a city, just a large sleepy town on the upper Mekong River. Its true name is Viang Chan, which means Rampart of Sandalwood, after the sixteenth-century city fortifications, but the tortured French pronunciation became "Vien Chin" when Laos became a French colony at the end of the nineteenth century.

Along the remarkably peaceful streets dozens of orange-robed Buddhists monks strolled with their gold-colored umbrellas. At first I could not figure out what was wrong, but then it dawned on me that I was missing the continuous Hanoi symphony of honking horns and whizzing motorbikes. An integral element of Vietnamese driving is honking every five seconds. The Lao, however, think this is just plain rude. There were certainly more cars in little Vientiane than in all of big Hanoi, but the Lao do not honk. The driving rules, or lack thereof, were about the same, but the Lao are much more patient than the Vietnamese. The Lao driver that Det 3 had arranged for me said that the only people who ever have wrecks in Vientiane are Vietnamese tourists. He suspected that people crashed into them just to stop their honking.

At the same time, the Vietnamese considered the Lao to be crude, backwoods, unrefined country cousins. While this is mostly true—the Lao are

Another golden Buddha, Vientiane, Laos.

Jumbo on the right, tuk-tuk on the left; Phang Kham Road, Vientiane, Laos.

Lan Xang Avenue dominated by the Patuxai, or Victory Gate, in the background; Vientiane, Laos.

hardheaded and neither handsome, graceful, refined, nor sophisticated, unlike the Vietnamese—at least they do not honk.

There were no taxis in Vientiane, but instead people moved about on three-wheeled, colorful motorbikes and minibuses with an open back, like Jeepnies in the Philippines, but much smaller. The ones with little wheels were called *tuk-tuk;* the shorter ones with big wheels were jumbos.

I do not think I had ever seen so many golden pagodas, called *wat,* in one place, not even in Hong Kong. Everywhere you turned there was an incredibly beautiful temple or wall. Lan Xang Avenue was dominated by the Patuxai Victory Gate, a massive Asian version of Paris's Arc de Triomphe, an ironic homage to the end of French colonial rule and commemorating Laos's independence.

Of all the markets I had been to in Asia, I found my favorite in the Talat Sao, or Morning Market, near the U.S. Embassy. I spent a good part of a day there because the minority tribes from the Lao-Vietnam-Thai border send to Talat Sao their best silver and silk crafts, which are of better quality and less expensive than what one finds in Hanoi. Very finely crafted, high-end artistic silver bracelets could be had for 100,000–300,000 *kip,* or ten to thirty dollars. Since my wife and daughter were coming to Hanoi for Christmas, I bought a dozen silver bracelets and a half-dozen silk scarves.

After a couple of days of business I had seen enough of Vientiane to be homesick for Hanoi and did not mind departing, this time on Vietnam Airlines.

A few months later I had to go to Phnom Penh, capital of the Royal Kingdom of Cambodia. The sophisticated, beautiful Vietnamese sneer at the Lao as ignorant country bumpkins, and in turn the Lao consider the Khmer of Cambodia as rubes. My Hanoi friends knew little about the place, and few would go there.

An old army buddy, Lt. Col. Mike Jaje, commanded Detachment 1 in Bangkok, Thailand. Although based in Thailand, Det 1 was responsible for doing MIA recovery missions in Cambodia, and Mike invited me to come over and see how they operate. For a couple of years he and I shared more than a few rough rides running military support to counterdrug operations on the Texas–New Mexico border. He and his wonderful wife, Dora, became dear friends of mine. Before going to Thailand they spent three years in Australia, where Mike was a liaison officer to the Australian army staff.

Our staff was somewhat concerned about the security situation in Cambodia, which had a mystique as the Asian Wild West. When I asked about it, Mike said it was no big deal, or at least it wasn't much worse than Laredo.

After a three-party election dispute the king of Cambodia had fled to Beijing, China, for health reasons, and members of each party in the contest were busy reducing the number of opposition party candidates by .45-caliber ballot. Since I wasn't running for office and the Cambodians weren't using high explosives to finalize the party tickets, I decided it would be fun to go; besides, I might learn a thing or two.

I had to first fly down to Saigon to change to a Vietnam Air Russian turboprop for the short leg up to Phnom Penh. As we approached for landing, I could see below a dry dusty plain that reminded me very much of West Texas. As I approached the customs counter I was immediately called by name and taken in hand by a well-dressed Khmer gentleman, who said very little but in a brisk walk steered me directly through customs and all of the usual bureaucratic formalities. At first I thought he might be Cambodian Internal Security and that we would now be going to the place where they experiment with forms of junior high science to get the answers they want.

He turned out to be Detachment 1's Cambodian handler, a career U.S. Air Force master sergeant. Although born in Phnom Penh, he had escaped as a teenager to the United States after Pol Pot and the great horror, so he knew intimately what had happened.

The following morning my trusty guide and mentor took me to the Toul Sleng High School, which the Communist Khmer Rouge had turned into the infamous prison camp S-21, which was preserved exactly as the Vietnamese had found it when they invaded and rescued Cambodia in 1979. I had been to Bergen-Belsen concentration camp in Germany, which was nothing like this, not even close. I was worldly, tough, and knowledgeable of human nature, including the worst of the intentions of humankind. What I saw at S-21 was nothing less than beastly. While I had some degree of historical sympathy for Vietnam's Viet Cong, at S-21 I developed a deep disgust for the Khmer Rouge.

A little insight that my guide gave me put it into perspective. The Khmer Rouge army consisted mostly of illiterate hill tribesmen with little understanding of the modern world or machinery. The day after they captured Phnom Penh, not a single car operated; all of the wheels were torn off, and the tires cut up to make rubber sandals for the army. This is true.

Given the incredible tragedy of their modern history, I was prepared to meet a hardened, grim, suspicious populace but in fact never saw a sign of this. One could never accuse the Khmer of being a pretty people, but I found them lighthearted, completely open and friendly, with a ready smile and hug, and plenty of music in the streets. Tet drums and the colorful dragon dancers went all around to chase away the spirits. The traffic was polite, even lazy, and, unlike in Viet Nam, the entire time I did not see a single "Mr. Pizza

Dragon dance, Preah Ang Phanauvong Street, Phnom Penh, Cambodia.

A new friend, the Sisowath Quay on the Mekong River, Phnom Penh, Cambodia.

Head," brains scattered in the road, various bent motorbike parts protruding from its torso.

Born at the intersection of the Bassac, Tonle Sap, and Mekong rivers, the origin of Phnom Penh is the Wat Phnom Daun Penh, or Hill Temple of Grandma Penh, the rich widow Penh, who built the fourteenth-century temple.

The central feature of Phnom Penh is Sisowath Quay, the mile-long stretch along the Mekong—the most beautiful part of the great river, a long, pleasant park, the palace, charming outdoor cafés and shops, and a carnival atmosphere. This is certainly the best of the three principal Mekong River cities, which include Vientiane to the north, Phnom Penh in the center, and

Saigon in the south, where the river meets the South China Sea fifty kilometers southwest of the city. Lazing on the quay in an outdoor pub while drinking a Lao Bao beer, I began thinking that someday I want to ride the mighty Mekong from China to the delta, only take a whole year.

Unlike anybody else in Asia, the Cambodians have very lyrical names—Sam Mom, Mony, Vanty, Srey, Rainsy—easy on the ear and the tongue.

I usually tried to visit with expats and tourists to get a good story, as in—so why are you here? In Cambodia the expats I found to be a generally tough lot; they were there because nobody else was. The tourists were none of your wide-eyed, innocent, spastic, tottering type but seasoned Asian hands who had been everywhere else and had come to the frontier, the more daring ones chatting about pushing on west into Burma. Likewise, after a while, they always asked for my story. We have a saying at the detachment—just give them the gospel of our search and leave them in tears. Needless to say, it usually struck a chord in the heart, and I was always proud to tell and be a part of it.

Chapter 8
CHASING ODYSSEUS

GOING INTO THE SEVENTY-FIFTH joint field activity in October 2003 I was feeling confident and knowledgeable about operations, having had considerable success my first three months in command. On my first JFA we had four successful recoveries, which eventually led to identification and return to families, including Captain Carl Long, a fellow Texas Aggie, from the Vung Tau site. In addition, we had the contingency turnover of Special Forces SFC Hanna and MSG Lindewald. I had always been lucky in operations and believed the gods and God were watching over me. Many Vietnamese believe in a variety of local gods, river spirits, jungle forces, and mountain gods, no different from the ancient Greeks. Who was I not to honor them? I needed all the help I could get.

Around this time Joint Task Force–Full Accounting was transformed into Joint POW/MIA Accounting Command (JPAC) by absorbing command and control of the Central Identification Laboratory and assuming a worldwide mission. Army Brigadier General W. Montague "Que" Winfield took command of the organization, an officer whom I came to greatly admire and respect during the following year.

With the teams coming in country in a week or so, Buddy and I took off to do joint advance work, checking three of the sites we intended to work that we had not had a chance to inspect. We generally tried to plan operations that followed the weather patterns. Since dry season in the north is from October through November, we planned to carry out much of the work in the upper part of the country at that time.

I was getting steeped in the lore of the mission and on the flight down to Hue heard some new stories from Buddy. At one time some tourists reported a live sighting of an African American in chains being guarded by Vietnamese with rifles near the Cambodian border. When the investigative team arrived, it found the descendent of a Senegalese French Foreign Legionnaire logging precious hardwood and using chains to drag the logs while armed guards protected his wood from thieves. Every live sighting requires an investigation. This was one of more than two hundred live sightings investigated, which never once produced credible evidence of live POWs still being held by Vietnam.

The CIL lab had a case in which all of the criteria and evidence were clear for an identification except that the myocardial DNA did not match. The lab eventually discovered that the mother had given false DNA because she did not want to know the truth. The ID was finally done with accurate DNA from the mother's sister.

Another ID was stymied for years because there were no living family members from which to draw a DNA sample. Finally the soldier's widow realized that technology had advanced to the point where DNA could probably be extracted from the thirty-year-old licked envelope seals of love letters she had saved. The ID was completed.

My favorite case was that of a retirement-eligible sergeant who boarded a plane in Saigon to return to the States but somehow was never put on the aircraft manifest. When he arrived in San Francisco with orders in hand for Fort Benning, he disappeared into the homeless street scene of the city for two decades. As far as the army knew, he was last seen in Saigon since there was no proof he had left Vietnam. He never arrived at Fort Benning and thus was an MIA. Twenty-four years later, he arrived at the front gate of Fort Benning, announced his name, and allowed that he might be in trouble. Eventually he was medically retired for a mental condition. Case closed.

We drove north from Hue's Phu Bai Airport, crossing the old DMZ and spending the night at Dong Hoi. Early the next morning we met our counterparts and headed west into the heart of Quang Binh province, where we parked as close as possible to the site. The remainder of the day would be consumed by a round-trip walk to the site and back.

It was a brutal hump, with at least five stream crossings, much of it under the last of the monsoon showers. This particular part of the Quang Binh jungle had very nasty leeches, but they provided an interesting insight in the difference in Eastern and Western thinking. To cross an area infested with leeches, the Vietnamese with us rolled up their pants legs, and all were wearing little sandals without socks. This way they could see when leeches latched on. When they spread Tiger Balm all over their legs, I asked whether that stopped the leeches. No, was the reply, but it made the bites hurt less.

I had on my waterproof Asolo boots and attached waterproof Gore-Tex leggings, which I had soaked in industrial-strength insect repellant. The Vietnamese laughed at my leggings and called me sissy-boy. I also had on ripstop nylon pants because your old leech will almost wiggle right through cotton. A half-hour later we were literally covered in leeches from the knees down. The Vietnamese were dancing round slapping and trying to pull them off, while I had the extreme pleasure of standing there watching because the leeches could not get under my leggings or in my boots and were having a mortal spasmodic reaction to the insect repellant.

When we finally got back to our vehicles, some of the Vietnamese asked where one might get these Asolo boots, Gore-Tex leggings, and this insect repellant. When I told them how much those things cost, they said forget it, it was much cheaper just to let them bite you.

We hustled back to Hanoi and grabbed one of the drivers to take us east to the South China Sea to Ha Long City, the port capital of Quang Ninh province on the Chinese border. There we met one of our twin-engine MI-17 helicopters for a visit to a site high above Ha Long Bay.

The aircraft strained and shuddered as we climbed higher and higher in the clouds and majestic karst mountains. When we finally approached the landing zone, I was astonished that the pilot was going to try to land. The LZ was a postage-stamp ledge cleared and carved out of the side of the mountain. The pilot hovered even with the ledge, slowly crabbing sideways until we were over the tiny spot of earth, the whirling blades inching terribly close to the cliff face bordering the LZ. After the aircraft settled and I could breathe again, I realized the pilot had probably made at least ten previous trips to this LZ, hauling supplies, as the base camp construction was well under way.

Negotiating a series of steep trails, I inspected the layout of the camp and the nearly finished bamboo structures, tent platforms, kitchen, workstation,

New Red Dao friend, Chinese border, Quang Ninh province. *Courtesy Buddy Newell*

Into the high mountains on the Chinese border in Quang Ninh province. Just behind me is Lt. Col. Tim Orner. *Courtesy Buddy Newell*

and screening stations, skillfully built by a group of Red Dao (Yao or Dzao) tribespeople. Intrigued by their colorful red-and-black dress, I asked some of the women whether they would take a picture with me. However, because they believe that the camera steals one's spirit, they refused. Finally, one said she wasn't afraid and came over. Soon the women made it clear to me that my new Red Dao girlfriend intended to be my next bride if some tragedy should befall my "principal" wife. I wondered whether the women were not beyond conspiring to help that tragedy along by casting spells with Dao magic to get a big cay thong tree to fall on Holly's head or a red cobra to bite her ankle. I intended to foil such a dastardly plot by giving Holly strict instructions while living in Pennsylvania to avoid cay thong trees and to keep an extra sharp eye out for red cobras.

The next morning we started by road for a round trip to a site well west of Hanoi, near the Lao border in Son La province. It was supposed to be a simple three-hour drive on good Route 6. Of course, we discovered at the last minute that Route 6 was closed due to blasting and improvements. So we had to go the only other route, way northwest through the mountains and then southwest through them, along three hundred kilometers of bad road and goat trails where sane people would never venture. We twice crossed the Song Da River on a rickety old ferry. It was fifteen hours of fun and some of the most incredible landscape I have ever seen.

At the end of the week the teams flew into Hanoi, and we spent a few days briefing the operations order, finalizing equipment loads, and acclimating before they scattered to sites in five different provinces. I would wait a week for their digs to get under way before Buddy and I followed up with our first series of site visits.

Buddy, our driver, Mr. Thinh, and I were preparing to go down Route 1 to the large site at Vinh when Mr. Tu of the VNOSMP called. He said we needed to launch a contingency operation to Ha Tinh province, where two farmers had found remains and material associated with a crash/burial case there. Ha Tinh was the next province below our site in Vinh, so we could stop there, pick up an anthro, and meet our counterparts.

The next morning, with anthro Derek Benedix in tow, we left Vinh for Ha Tinh City, following the VNOSMP van. I read the case file on the way down. It was a 1966 crash of an air force F-105D with a single pilot. Local villagers had buried the remains, but the witnesses were unreliable. Since 1993 JTF-FA had done six investigations and three recovery digs at the site but had found no remains.

As we approached the little farming hamlet, I noticed a squad of Vietnamese police scattered along the treeline, more on the other side of the hamlet, and a van full waiting for us at the home of one of the two farmers. In the yard were also district officials and local villagers. When I asked Mr. Tu, "Why all the police?" he shrugged, as surprised as I was. He suggested that perhaps the police were just a precaution. We were greeted by the two young farmers, who led us behind the house and across a dry rice field, the crowd and police following. Reaching a patch of tall grass, they pulled a small, brightly colored Vietnamese coffin from its hiding place.

I ask whether this was where they had found the remains. No, they said, a few fields over, near the pond. I ask whether they would open the box and allow Derek to examine the contents. Wordlessly, one gently pulled back the lid. I could see part of a pilot's G-suit mixed with the remains. After asking for permission to photograph, Derek laid out the contents and began snapping, doing a careful examination as he worked. "Are they Asian?" I asked quietly. "No, Western, probably Caucasian," he whispered.

An old woman with an angry look suddenly drew near, waggling her finger at the two young men and speaking in a firm voice. Buddy had a pained look on his face. Leaning toward me, she was saying that she was not going to allow them to turn over those remains to the authorities and would stomp on the bones if we tried to take them. In a calm voice I asked her whether she understood that this would bring long-sought answers to a grieving mother, widow, and family on the other side of the world. Beginning to cry, the old woman asked, what about *my* answers? My husband was a soldier, too, and missing from the war. Go find him, and then you can have this one. Who would bring back *my* child, who was killed by American bombs? she sobbed.

Buddy turned to me and said he had just overheard someone in the crowd say she was the mother of those two young farmers. I knew instantly there would not be a turnover today. I decided to salvage what we could by getting as much information as possible, especially exactly where they had found the remains.

I asked one of the young farmers to show me where they had dug up the bones. He nodded, beckoning me to follow. I told Buddy to keep talking to her and said that we would be back. Derek and I followed the farmer at a clipped pace across several fields, arriving near an old barn close to the pond that had been a central landmark for previous digs. Rounding the barn, we came to a large garden. On its edge was a three-foot hole in the ground, and above the hole a glittering, makeshift shrine complete with burning joss sticks. I was very touched by the shrine. They had obviously accidentally uncovered the long-lost burial while planting something in the garden. Derek whipped out his camera and illegal GPS, recording landmarks, pacing back to the hole from three directions for triangulation, and calling out to me the bearing and distance as I hastily sketched a map.

When we had finished mapping, I looked up and realized we were completely alone. We had no interpreter, no VNOSMP counterparts, no cops. Even the farmer had disappeared. I didn't mind at all; it was liberating. However, I knew Mr. Tu was going to be upset because he was responsible if some misfortune should waylay us.

Making our way back to the small coffin and the crowd, we arrived to find Buddy and Mr. Tu practically surrounded by villagers, the cops looking very nervous, and the old woman still crying. I was gathering a sense of the crowd dynamics when suddenly an old man wandered up, obviously very intoxicated. He began to harangue the villagers, shouting, shaking his fist, spitting, and stomping the ground after each outburst. The faces in the crowd turned very hostile as they listened to the old man. I had no idea what he was saying, but I tapped Mr. Tu on the shoulder to indicate that it was time to leave—now. He nodded, and as calmly as we could, we walked back toward our waiting vehicles, where Mr. Tu politely admonished me for disappearing. Buddy claimed I had cast him to the wolves and run away.

I told Mr. Tu we had determined the exact location of the burial and that I believed the two young farmers were very decent and honest and were trying to do the right thing, but their mother was the major obstacle. I believed if we waited a few months for things to calm down, the young men could probably be persuaded to bring the remains into the district office, well away from the mother and the hostile village. Agreeing, he promised to talk to the local officials.

In December 2004 these remains were finally turned over to the Vietnamese authorities and subsequently to the U.S. MIA Office for repatriation. In October 2005 CIL identified USAF Colonel Eugene D. "Dave" Hamilton, from Pepperall, Alabama. Hamilton was a thirty-two-year-old captain when he was shot down in his F-105 on January 31, 1966. He had been flying on his eighty-seventh mission with the 469th Tactical Fighter Squadron out of Korat Royal Thai Air Force Base in Thailand. In June 2006 Colonel Hamilton was buried in Arlington National Cemetery.

Disappointed at not securing a remains turnover, we returned to Vinh in time for a remarkable evening. The knock at my door was our explosive ordnance disposal specialist, a U.S. Marine Corps gunnery sergeant, who invited me to the hotel lobby to join in the traditional celebration of the birthday of the corps. I arrived to find a large cake adorned with the USMC globe and anchor, the recovery team in solemn formation, and their special guests, a half-dozen cute Japanese dental hygienists who were in Vinh doing humanitarian clinics. We sang the Marine Corps hymn while Gunny, not having a proper NCO sword, cut the cake with a Vietnamese machete. It was a bit surreal, celebrating this auspicious occasion in the birthplace of Ho Chi Minh, with Japanese guests politely trying to sing along. It had to be one of the most unique birthdays in the history of the corps. That night I sent an e-mail account to Major Tom Dicken, my marine executive officer, who was profoundly jealous to have missed it.

Buddy and I returned north to grab a helicopter to fly back out to the recovery site in beautiful Son La province, west of Hanoi near the Lao border. The dig was in a communal tea plantation, and we had gone around and around with the Vietnamese team leader, Senior Colonel Pham Cong Khoi, over the price per bush of the tea we had to pull up. He insisted this was not ordinary Vietnamese tea, for which we pay a few dollars a plant, but was very special, ancient, imported, extremely valuable Chinese tea. We sent a sample to a tea expert, who confirmed Colonel Khoi's claim and also gave us a typical world price estimate, which was four times what Colonel Khoi was asking us to pay the commune. Although a tough old soldier, Pham Cong Khoi was always honest and had a ready smile and a grand sense of humor. I had grown to like and respect him.

Son La province, along the Song Da River.

Screening station, tea plantation site, Moc Chau, Son La province.

When our MI-17 touched down in Moc Chau, the local school turned out to watch the helicopter land, kids lining the landing zone and waving furiously. Senior Colonel Khoi was there to greet me. With a perfectly straight face I told him I had come to finalize the price and pick up the thousand tea plants I had to buy for clearing the site. To pay for the expense, I explained, Buddy Newell was going to have to spend every day selling baskets of this tea in the street in front of the detachment in Hanoi with the other women there, who were selling limes, oranges, and mangoes. I enjoyed the moment while I watched Colonel Khoi and his assistants go into a serious huddle to figure out whether the *ông* was kidding or not. they came out laughing, but I never cracked a smile.

This led to a long lunch to negotiate the price of tea in the yard of one of the commune farmers. We sat in tiny plastic chairs at a tiny table while several women brought out a five-course meal cooked over a propane burner. I am still not sure what we ate, but some of it was wonderful. After the meal Colonel Khoi brought out a stack of tiny teacups with a Le Vie water bottle full of *cuoc lui,* which roughly translates as "go secretly to the still," which in Texas is called white lighting or tanglefoot. Knowing we had a hard-and-fast rule of not drinking during duty hours, Colonel Khoi proclaimed, "We shall now have tea!" He filled each of the tiny teacups from his Le Vie bottle, and we began negotiations Vietnamese style.

Each official at the table made a polite speech, which required a toast. The clever Colonel Khoi kept our teacups full, and his own speech got at least three toasts each time he pretended to conclude. Having the last word,

I offered appropriate remarks about the new spirit of cooperation and the mutual future interest of our two nations. I closed by agreeing to the price of the tea plants, letting them off the hook about Buddy having to sell tea in the street in front of the detachment building. I was not sure who was more relieved, Colonel Khoi or Buddy.

We sat for a long while chatting in good spirits in the farmer's yard. I scanned the incredibly white karst hills jutting from the landscape, the clean deep green of the tea plants surrounding us in the crisp air, hearing an innate harmony of the sirens' lullaby, a powerful sense of serenity, of permanence. Like Homer's lotus eaters, I wanted to linger forever to watch the sunsets and the rising moon. Three times Buddy warned me we had to take

Dig site, tea plantation, Moc Chau, Son La province.

Negotiations over the price of tea plants on a local farmer's back porch, Moc Chau, Son La province. Far left corner: Capt. Dave Emmons, the team leader; in the right corner beside me is Buddy Newell. In the left center is Senior Col. Pham Cong Khoi.

off immediately to make Hanoi by dark. Finally, reluctantly, I strolled toward the waiting helicopter.

Our good fortune continued throughout most of the month of site visits. Up on the Chinese border, above Ha Long Bay, Dr. "Hoss" Moore finally closed that much-worked, difficult site. Flying off the USS *Kitty Hawk* in an A-6A Intruder from Fighter Attack Squadron 52 (VA-52) on August 20, 1972, U.S. Navy Lieutenant Harry S. Mossman, from Manhasset, New York, was flying a night mission to strike Da Mon Toi when he failed to return. Lieutenant Mossman's remains were identified by CIL in May 2004, and he was buried in Tahoma National Cemetery in August 2004.

Down in Quang Tri province, near Lang Vei Special Forces Camp, U.S. Army Captain Ryan Wolfgram and his investigative team surveyed a site looking for the A-1 Skyraider pilot who went missing in February 1968 while going after the PAVN tanks attacking the camp. Ryan turned up a dogtag and bits of blue cockpit glass distinctive of the A-1 Skyraider of the period. This led to four recovery operations, 2004–2006, which ultimately resulted in the October 2007 burial in Arlington National Cemetery of USAF Major Robert G. Lapham of Marshall, Michigan. Shot down on February 8, 1968, the forty-year-old Lapham had been flying out of Pleiku with the 1st Air Commando Squadron when he earned a posthumous Silver Star for attacking the NVA tanks at Lang Vei.

The Vinh site became a huge rock in our rucksack. The team had come almost a month early to oversee the complex engineering and construction and remained a month after the other teams had returned to Hawaii. The project was monumental in both scale and scope inasmuch as the team had to pull five tons of airplane out of a pond in the middle of a city.

After rerouting the city power and phone lines over the site, the Vietnamese construction company, a converted Vietnamese army engineer regiment having to earn its keep, brought in a huge crane to pile-drive twelve-meter interlocking steel plates to form a box around the pond. In theory the deep steel box would prevent the walls of the pond from collapsing as we dug, thus preventing the foundations of the surrounding housing from sloughing and giving way as the pond drained. The procedure actually worked pretty well.

I was more concerned with the safety of the team and the workers in the bottom of the twenty-foot hole because, if the walls collapsed, they would drown or be buried under the mud. To mitigate this, on the inside we built a steel I-beam skeleton support for the interior of the walls. The skeleton could be lowered as the team worked downward, while a huge marine pump kept the site drained. To dig the site we put away the trowels and shovels and brought in bucket loaders, front-end loaders, and dump trucks.

Over the weeks the tail of the aircraft slowly began to emerge, then the engine. With mounting anticipation the team carefully worked downward through the mud toward the front of the aircraft, which abruptly ended at the leading edge of the engine blades. The long metal probes, test bore holes, and EOD metal detectors made it clear that the area below the engine was sterile: There was no cockpit. I watched as the crane lifted the massive tail and engine out of the hole.

It was possible the cockpit had sheared off at impact and was still buried somewhere under the neighborhood. There was another possibility as well. At the time of the crash this was a new type of aircraft with state-of-the-art avionics. The cockpit could be gathering dust in some aviation warehouse in Moscow.

I stood at the edge of the site and glared into the cavernous hole. Where was the cockpit? I demanded. Where was the pilot? I wanted to shout, furious with God and the gods. Speak to me! The stalwart young men and women of the recovery team had endured tremendous hardships and made every sacrifice asked of them. My appeals to the cosmos were met with silence.

I turned to Capt. Eric Lanham and Dr. Pete Miller, the anthro. The look in their eyes told me there was nothing else to be done for now. I told them to shut down the site and take the team back to Hawaii. I asked Mr. Tu to inform the local officials that they could start the environmental reclamation project we had funded for the site.

It was a crushing blow to the morale of the recovery team. I explained to them the benefit they had brought by safely executing a very complex mission without harm to themselves, the workers, or the surrounding buildings. The neighborhood fears of unexploded ordnance in the pond had been laid to rest. Part of the mystery was solved: We knew where the cockpit was not. Each team member had been a model ambassador by demonstrating the fine qualities of Americans to the local residents, many of whom were still bitter about the war. Their efforts had not been for naught.

The recovery site in Vinh, Nghe An province.

Vinh, Nghe An province.

Vinh, Nghe An province.

As we drove back up Route 1 to Hanoi, my disappointment slowly morphed into a more positive reflection on what we had actually achieved in the past two months, not the tactical aspects but the strategic and political ones. A joint field activity usually lasts only thirty days, four times a year. But we were seeing new developments in United States–Vietnam relations just in the past month or so. The Vietnamese foreign minister met with ours, their minister of defense went to the United States to meet with ours, and the U.S. Navy made the first U.S. ship visit since the war. At the Vung Tau site during the last JFA, the Vietnamese had let us bring in some of the team early to prepare the site and allowed them to stay several extra weeks to finish. The same thing occurred with the Vinh site. I wanted to press the situation as far as possible and to take advantage of this new, developing relationship.

Typically, the Vietnamese team leader oversaw most of the advance work—constructing base camps and workstations and cutting trails—while Buddy and I went from site to site checking the work progress during the joint advance work (JAW) phase. Often things did not get done exactly as we had planned, not through lack of effort but through miscommunication. I decided in the future we would press for a seven- or ten-day early arrival of at least the team sergeant, a linguist, and a medic to oversee the preparation of each site. This would improve site-prep efficiency and reduce setup time when the full team arrived, thus adding to the number of possible dig days.

As an eternal optimist, by the time we reached the outskirts of Hanoi I was joking and laughing with Buddy again. Someday, I assured myself, we would find that cockpit.

We arrived back in Hanoi just in time for Thanksgiving 2003. The U.S. Defense attaché, Col. Steve Ball and his wife, Allaine, had all of the thirteen or so U.S. military in Hanoi to their house for turkey and potluck. Over the years a routine had developed with the detachment and the spouses of the U.S. Embassy staff. Much of our Det equipment, such as pumps and other machinery, was stored and serviced in Thailand, where the Bangkok Det kept a large warehouse. We moved the equipment back and forth on U.S. Air Force cargo aircraft.

We had evolved an informal system in which the embassy wives faxed their grocery orders to the commissary that serves the large U.S. Embassy in Bangkok. The commissary manager filled the orders, boxed them up, and drove them out to load our cargo plane. For some reason it was called the "channel flight." I was never sure which channel it was supposed to cross. When the plane landed in Hanoi, it was greeted by the women and their drivers, who sorted out the groceries while our logistics officer, Daniel Young, and his workers unloaded our equipment. As one might imagine, the timing of the channel flight just before Thanksgiving and Christmas was especially important. This wonderful informal relationship led to many home-cooked meals for members of the detachment, which I, as Det commander, considered essential to its morale.

Chapter 9
CHRISTMAS AND TET

I HAD DEVELOPED SUCH a spiritual fondness for the city that I was giving strong consideration to retiring in Hanoi and living somewhere near Hoan Kiem Lake or the old Hang Gai district with its warren of twisting streets and shops. On my long walks on Hai Ba Trung Street or Le Thai To and in talking to my expat friends, I started keeping an eye out for apartments or houses that might be coming available.

The whole idea suddenly became problematic, at least for a good while longer, with a brief e-mail congratulation from a friend in the Pentagon. Congratulations for what? I wrote. You made the colonel's promotion list, he shot back. That was a bolt out of the blue; promotion to full colonel was the last thing on my mind. At least it proved the army had a sense of humor. But it did mean about a year's wait to pin on and three years of service after that to keep the rank and retirement pay.

Christmas 2003 and Tet 2004 were fast approaching, and I was looking forward to a short break. Tet is the Vietnamese New Year, and the entire country shuts down for a week. Just before Christmas I had to go to the Det commanders' conference in Hawaii, where I would meet my wife, Holly, who would return with me to Hanoi for a few weeks. Our daughter, Dustin, who was going to college in Texas, would fly into Hanoi from San Antonio.

I had been to Hawaii many times, but for Holly it was a first trip to the Pacific. I met her at the Honolulu Airport with traditional flower leis, and we drove to stay at the Hale Koa, the military resort on Waikiki Beach.

The commanders' conference was very productive as we focused on fine-tuning our systems and functions. Brigadier General "Que" Winfield, our new boss, was set on upgrading our logistics, especially the tools we used on digs. Since JPAC and its healthy resources had taken over responsibility for the CIL lab, he agreed to finance the purchase of the highest-quality tools. Nothing was more frustrating to the teams than trying to do digs with cheap tools, especially trowels, shovels, root cutters, and chainsaws. He turned loose Lt. Col. Jay Orner, the JPAC J4, or logistics officer. Soon our warehouses were stuffed with the very best, Marshalltown trowels, Craftsman and Dewalt tools, and Poulan chainsaws. The anthros all applauded this new, direct-command interest in the tools of their trade.

In our free time Holly and I did the normal tourist trek. The USS *Arizona* Memorial was very moving, with its eerie oil bubbles bleeding to the surface, like black teardrops of angels spread in the sunlight, giving off rainbow colors. Probably the highlight was snorkeling with sea turtles in the Hanauma Bay Nature Preserve.

We were on separate flights back to Bangkok and in different terminals for the mandatory long layover at Tokyo's Narita Airport. The real problem was that Holly got into Bangkok's Suvarnabhumi Airport several hours before I did, her first experience at dealing with Asian customs entry, although Thailand is relatively easy and friendly. I decided the simplest plan was to have a room at the Amari, an excellent hotel right in the airport. She also had the phone number of the detachment in Thailand, so I knew if anything went wrong, she could get plenty of help. As it turned out, she breezed right through the entire trip as planned.

The next morning we flew together on Vietnam Air into Hanoi, where we were met by a smiling Mr. Thinh. I think the rest of Christmas and New Years is better told through Holly's eyes, new to Asia, in her notes back home to the family:

> The flight was tough, sitting on planes for hours and hours, but we are finally here in Hanoi, which is fascinating. We only just arrived Monday afternoon, and my impression so far of the city is a combination of Mexico and East Berlin poverty, French colonial elegance, big-city traffic and crowds. Coming from the airport I saw water buffalo, peasants in traditional dress, men and women in business suits, fashionable clothing, and beautiful new homes next to hovels. I think shopping is going to be great—just think, East Berlin prices but more choices of good quality. It's too soon to tell.

Ty is at work downstairs now, but we are going to lunch and then do a little exploring later. Getting around will be much easier because if we are not going to be close enough to walk, Ty will have a driver or taxi take us.

It has already been a little stressful because I had to meet all of the staff and help. I'm still suffering a little from jet lag, so learning names is going to be tough, and all the Vietnamese cleaning ladies wanted to practice their limited English with me. I can't understand a word they say, so I'm nodding and smiling a lot.

I feel as though I am in an old Bogart movie. There are a lot of foreign "characters" that live here. Ty and I ate at a neat little restaurant last night owned by a Canadian. I need to get Ty to tell me his story later. There are apparently a lot of stories here.

Ty's apartment is quite comfortable, but I feel weird being a guest in my husband's "home." I don't have anything to do; he has a cook and four cleaning ladies. The laundry fairy magically has your dirty clothes washed, ironed, and put away without you ever knowing it was done. The place itself is elegant, but when you look a little closer, you start seeing the flaws and shoddy construction. Still, it's located on a beautiful lake, and the view is spectacular.

Hawaii was nice, but I feel I have now been there, don't need to come back except if we stayed on another island on the beach without all the tourist crowds and high-rise hotels. We liked Key West more. If you just want beach and surf, go to the Bahamas; it's cheaper, and you don't have the long flight.

I am surprised by the number of Westerners that are on vacation here in Vietnam. Apparently the word is out that this is definitely the place to come if you want someplace exotic where your money will stretch as far as possible. Ty was right, the shopping is very good, and there are a lot of comfortable hotels in the city. More adventures as well, such as the trip to Sa Pa.

Our Sa Pa trip began late at night with an overnight train ride to Lao Cai. The guests of the hotel, the Victoria, ride in a luxurious private sleeping car. It's all very surreal because this four-star hotel is located in the isolated village called Sa Pa near the Chinese border. There are a number of minority tribes living in the area, and the scenery is breathtaking, so it is becoming a popular tourist area. When we arrived in our train berth, we found colorful embroidered bags that contained a bottle of water, washcloth, toothbrush, and toothpaste. We all slept well on the train, although I woke up a few times and could tell we were traveling up a steep winding track into the

Holly and Dustin Smith, Hai Ba Trung Street, Hanoi.

Red Dao woman and child, Ta Phin village, near Sa Pa, Lao Cai province on the Chinese border.

Black H'mong at the market, Sa Pa, Lao Cai province.

The far northern border with China, Lao Cai province.

mountains. The train only goes as far as the village of Lao Cai, and then we had to take a hotel van up a very steep road to Sa Pa.

After checking into this wonderful hotel in the middle of nowhere, changing into warmer clothes, eating a fabulous buffet breakfast catered to all tastes—Asian, European, American, Hispanic, Ty hired a driver and guide.

We visited a very small village, Ta Phin, of the Red Dao (Zow) people, which was even higher in the mountains and closer to China. When we arrived, we were immediately surrounded by the women and children, dressed in wonderful, colorful costumes and red turbans. Dustin brought along a gyroscope and a harmonica and was therefore very popular with the crowd of children. After a long walk into the village and up into the hills, we were invited into one of their huts, which was very dark and smoky, but it was interesting, to say the least. Dustin sat at the fire with the young girls, Ty and I sat on a crude bench. It was so dark you could barely see. The women, and especially the young girls, have learned English fairly well and began a dialogue in order to convince you to "buy something from me."

They ask your name, how many children you have, how old you are, is this my husband, daughter, etc.? They hope this will put a spell on you, and you will not resist the urge to buy their stuff. It works; I now have many "sisters." Ty, Dustin, and I helped the Vietnam economy quite a bit by purchasing a lot of their handcrafted items.

We returned to Sa Pa in the afternoon and went to the Sunday weekend market, which was packed with Dao, Giay, and Hmong villagers, who were selling food, crafts, and supplies. We were again surrounded, this time by

Ha Long Bay, Quang Ninh province, a World Heritage site.

tiny ladies from the Tay minority dressed in dark indigo. Their hands are blue from the dye. They also would not leave you alone. They found a great customer in Dustin. The next morning we spent a leisurely morning exploring the streets of Sa Pa. That doesn't take long.

Dustin was suffering a bit from either the water or something she ate, so stayed near the hotel, but Ty and I hiked down into a beautiful valley to see a waterfall, bridge, and stroll through the village of Cat Cat. It was an hour hike down into the valley, but we were rewarded with spectacular views. The hump up was pretty hard, but halfway up on the return you meet the road and the young men with motorbikes, who are happy to give you a lift back to Sa Pa for 10,000 *dong*, about a dollar. We would have happily paid double that or more. I think Ty would have paid any price just to see me riding on the back of a motorbike up that winding road.

We left Sa Pa on Monday evening to take a jeep down to the train station. We were rather apprehensive about the drive because the fog at Sa Pa was very thick, and it is a pretty scary road even in the daylight. Oh well, just one more adventure, so we pressed on. Luckily we came out from the clouds soon, and our driver was the exception to most Vietnamese drivers, slow and careful. We got to the train on time and arrived back in Hanoi at 4:30 in the morning. After showering and breakfast we had a leisurely New Year's day.

Shortly after this I took the ladies out two hours east of Hanoi to Ha Long Bay, a World Heritage site, with starkly beautiful karst peaks rising up in a series of watery mazes in a blue-green bay on a bouncing boat. The ladies turned up their noses at lunch of unidentifiable substances aboard the boat, but I was polite and asked before I stuck my chopsticks into their plates to suck up any and all consumables that might go to waste on such delicate appetites. While doing so I was thinking of a joke: At a beach in Vietnam, if someone yells "Shark!" everyone runs into the water.

A few days later, after a long, taxing flight they were safely back in the States, with an entirely new view of the universe, which was the most important point and the best Christmas gift I could give.

Tet, the Vietnamese celebration of the New Year, usually comes between mid-January and early February, depending on the lunar calendar. For a week the country, including stores and restaurants, entirely shuts down, and even taxis were hard to find. Homes and businesses were brightly decorated; the colorful kumquat bush with its bright orange fruit was on display everywhere. The ritual, called *Le Tru Tich,* is believed to bring good luck for the year. Beginning just before midnight as the year turns, the celebration involves an incredible din of gongs and fireworks.

With Holly and Dustin returned stateside and most of the staff gone, I spent most of the week alone at the detachment, reading and puttering around the building. I was relieved to see the end of Tet so we could go back to the mission.

It was about this time, in January 2004, that I discovered Dr. Tran Thanh Huong and traditional oriental medicine. After badly injuring the muscles in my right forearm from a fall on a rock the previous year, I had been in pain. While I was at the Army War College, the sports medicine specialists had given the muscles a shot of some steroid cocktail, which improved it from intense pain to merely a constant annoyance.

One day when Buddy saw me putting ice on the arm, he mentioned that I should try this Vietnamese doctor who treats many of the ambassadors and Western executives. She had an exclusive client list, but Major Tom Dicken knew her and perhaps could arrange an introduction.

With a little trepidation about what I was getting myself into, I had my first session with Dr. Huong. She was a very interesting woman who had been educated in France. She had practiced standard Western medicine for many years before focusing on traditional oriental practices. She spoke four languages, and her husband was also a doctor who worked for the United Nations in Rome.

Saying that she couldn't promise anything and that I probably should have let the specialists from Walter Reed Hospital operate like they wanted to do, but if I was willing, she would give it a try. She had a very pleasant, happy nature, laughing with me while turning my arm into a porcupine and hooking up a little voltage box that made my arm muscle twitch for twenty minutes. To my surprise, the needles and the treatment were nearly painless.

While I was lying on the table, a young man came into the clinic and explained in Spanish that he was a doctor from Spain, was studying oriental medicine, and knew all about Dr. Huong. He asked her to please let him hang around her clinic and observe for a few weeks. His endorsement sent the needle on my confidence meter up, but she politely sent the poor guy packing, saying, also in Spanish, that her patients guarded their privacy and that they would probably be upset with a stranger about.

She returned to my table to complete the session, asking if everything was okay. I answered in Spanish, which she seemed to think was very amusing. More important, it gave her great face with me because she knew that I knew what had just happened with the Spaniard when she was determined to protect her clients. She slapped on an oriental herb poultice called *thien huony,* which I had to keep on the arm until the next afternoon.

When I returned for my second session, Dr. Huong again put a half-dozen needles in my arm and one in the crown of my head, which immediately made me relaxed and sleepy. She brought out a big white cigar and lit it, waving it just above my injured area until it warmed up the skin. She kept directing the smoke down on my arm. She wanted me to breathe in the smoke for protection against the flu. I was a little hesitant, but later, when I came to completely trust her, I would do whatever she instructed. The "cigar" was a moxa leaf wrapped around the herb artemesia, and the therapy was moxibustion.

On the end of my finger she placed a ring attached to a long wire with a sharp probe, explaining she had to find and map the path from my right ear to my injured muscle through the meridians and collaterals of my body. When she touched exactly the correct spot on my ear, she said, I would feel a sharp little pain, the pain of my right arm resting in my ear.

She seemed a little perplexed when I denied feeling any pain at all in my right ear from her probing. Shaking her head and consulting her ear chart, she suddenly brightened and with a big smile went around to my left ear, the opposite side from my injured arm, and told me my internal wires were crossed. Owww! She got it exactly on first touch, like a wasp sting on my left ear. This made her very happy. She told me not to be concerned about having my internal wires crossed because this sometimes happens. I asked whether it made me special. No, she said, it just made her job more complicated.

I had to go on the road and couldn't come back for another session for a week. No problem, she explained. She would leave two tiny needles stuck in my ear and show me how to pull them out in three days. They looked like little buttons, almost invisible.

The arm was feeling better after only two sessions, and I was pain free in six. By then I had become a true believer, intensely interested, and during my sessions peppered her with questions about the philosophy and various therapies associated with traditional medicine. She brought out a manuscript, a small book she had written explaining the basics to her more curious patients and for the classes she taught to Western doctors. She knew from our conversations that I had published a half-dozen history books and asking whether I would edit it for spelling and proper English before it went to press.

That editing process provided me a grand opportunity to expand my horizons. The rough-and-tumble life in the detachment produced a number of other injuries, and, by the end of my tour, lying on a table with needles, suction cups, and a smoking moxa stick, all trying to balance the disorder of my meridians and collaterals, seemed perfectly normal.

Chapter 10

"THAT IS SOOOOO VIETNAM"

AS TET ENDED IN MID-JANUARY 2004, we entered into a hectic schedule preparing for the seventy-sixth joint field activity, which would be conducted from mid-February to mid-March 2004. We held the provincial coordination meeting in Dalat, the famous French colonial mountain retreat developed in the 1920s. The charming town in the Central Highlands is perched above Xuan Huong Lake and the Dalat market, above which runs a string of little cafés serving local coffee. Our meeting was in the dowager Empress Hotel, which has a commanding view of the lake and mountains and rooms still holding on to their elegant touch.

After Dalat we rushed back to Hanoi, conducted a repatriation ceremony at Noi Bai Airport, and returned to the detachment to pack and go south again the next morning.

Miss Tam, the cook, came to find me, reporting we were down to our last egg. Because of a new outbreak of avian flu, the government had initiated very strict control on all birds that might pick up the H5 virus. It was no longer possible to buy or order chicken anywhere, which was no great loss to me, but then Buddy added that the government had just announced that pork might also be infected with H5, so in a week there would probably be no bacon or pork chops at the market.

The avian flu was a very serious threat. The virus jumped from wild birds to domestic fowl, primarily chickens and ducks, the virtual staple of Vietnam, and at least eight Vietnamese people so far had died of the infection. By this time we knew the transmission was through direct skin contact with fowl feces, such as by walking barefoot in a farmyard. The danger was that the H5 virus would be picked up by someone already carrying a typical human flu and that the two would join, mutate, and become a contagious, airborne, lethal virus that would create a pandemic, making the Spanish influenza of 1918 seem like an outbreak of the common cold. The Spanish influenza killed ten million people. Many of my scientific friends believed it was a matter of when, not if.

The Vietnamese government ordered the immediate slaughter of tens of thousands of chickens and ducks and sent out the army and the police to ensure it was done. It also issued an edict declaring that all pet songbirds must be immediately destroyed by their owners. If anyone knew of a neighbor still keeping birds, the information had to be reported to the authorities.

The Vietnamese love to keep songbirds in little bamboo cages, and it is not unusual to see a cluster of cages on a tiny balcony. The destruction edict was sternly announced by blaring loudspeakers on every other street corner. By sundown the sky over Hanoi was filled with brightly colored songbirds. Most of them didn't know where to go, so they hung around in the trees near their owner's house. With a half-dozen living in our trees, we could hear the bird music at breakfast. There were songbirds flying and singing all over town. Buddy finished his breakfast *phuo,* shaking his head, "That is sooooo Vietnam."

We flew straightaway down to Saigon to start the long series of site visits for joint advance work before the teams flew in from Hawaii. After a week we had worked our way back to Da Nang for a final reconnaissance trip to a remote site in Quang Nam province, southwest of Da Nang.

Buddy, our operations officer, Sergeant Philip Revell, and I reached the tiny village of the Co Tu tribe by a long helicopter ride and a bumpy truck drive along a loopy dirt road. The entire village turned out to watch us meet our guide, a seventy-seven-year-old, chain-smoking Co Tu monk wearing flip-flops, an ankle-length wool topcoat, and a funny little wedding hat. I never did find out why he wore a wedding hat.

The site was just a short walk, the monk explained, waving his hand vaguely in the direction of the mountain behind the village. Leaving the truck and village behind, I was the only one carrying water and food, strictly adhering to the old infantry adage—never get separated from your rucksack.

Quang Nam province, southwest of Da Nang. Our guide is a Co Tu monk. *Courtesy Buddy Newell*

Hour two: just a little farther. *Courtesy Buddy Newell*

Four kilometers and an hour later, atop the first 1,800-foot hill, we began to suspect things were not going as we had imagined. Just a little farther, insisted our guide.

At the end of a second hour the good trail evaporated into dense jungle and a boulder-strewn creek that we crossed time and again. Soaking wet, bleeding from the wait-a-minute vines and sawgrass cuts, we dutifully followed the old Co Tu deeper into the tangle and higher up the slopes, pausing only now and then to wait for him or one of the Co Tu boys who had tagged along to wander off and check one of their many animal snares.

Much of the character of Vietnam is shaped by the daily struggle to survive in a cruel world. It was not then an impoverished nation, but it had been

Hour four, Buddy Newell and S.Sgt. Philip Revell check a GPS to see whether we are still in Vietnam.

Hour five: The site is just up there, not far. *Courtesy Buddy Newell*

in the not-so-distant past, so no one misses an opportunity to fill the larder and will eat anything that crawls, walks, or flies. I have spent entire days in the jungle seeing perhaps only a single bird, lizard, or snake, all of which were quickly dispatched for the hotpot lunch by the nimble guides.

As we struggled up yet another vine-choked hill, Buddy's foot went through a rotten log, exposing two enormous grubs the size of tea saucers. All giggles, the two Co Tu boys asked me to please share. Sure, I said, I'm not hungry today, and the grubs disappeared like fat white doughnuts into the boys' smiling faces. I was always glad for the chance to make children happy.

After every half hour we looked hopefully at the old monk guide. He beamed, saying *vâng vâng!* (sure, very soon now, very close). Finally, blessedly, the old man stopped and announced that we could see the site, just there by the big rock and the white tree. We followed his finger. Sure enough, we could see it, about two thousand feet higher and probably another hour's climb. We looked into each other's exhausted faces and stood quietly for a long while just staring up at the mountaintop. Finally, one of us broke the silence in a world-weary deadpan, "That issss sooooo Vietnam."

I returned to Hanoi with Band-Aids and bruises in odd places and a set of expensive L.L. Bean shirt and pants that were completely ruined. Miss My came by my apartment to take away the laundry. I shook the clothes out of my backpack. She held her nose and picked them up with a long stick.

When the teams flew into Da Nang in late February 2004 and we met for the operations order, I explained that the seventy-sixth JFA was going to be a thirty-day exercise in maneuver warfare and that flexibility was key to success. I wanted to open eight sites, not the usual five. We had succeeded in the prep-work proof of concept by bringing in ten days early the assistant team sergeants to supervise the preparation of two sites, one in the far south, on the coast of Kien Giang province near the Cambodian border, and another in western Nghe An province on the Lao border. Those two sites were ready to go and would be worked by the same teams during the entire joint field activity.

The remaining six sites each entailed relatively short work, either a few days or a week to finally close a site worked earlier and suspended or to undertake new sites that were very focused and would require no more than fifteen days to open and complete. The teams knew on which sites they would start but not which one I would send them to next, depending on who was ready to move on and when. Above all, we could not compromise scientific thoroughness for speed. I knew this concept was also going to test the flexibility of our Vietnamese counterparts, who had agreed to the plan in principle but, I thought, had not quite comprehended the intent or the pace of operations I expected.

In the end they were more flexible than I had imagined, although my counter part, Mr. Tu, half in jest complained that in the process I had had completely worn out every American and Vietnamese involved. When one of the teams indicated it was within a few days of closing, I would tell the Vietnamese team chief which site they would do next, dashing him off to complete the preparations for that site. We opened eight sites, closed seven, and suspended one, which would be completed during the next joint field activity in April and May. More important, we recovered the remains of three MIA.

On the coast of Kien Giang province near the Cambodian border, Capt. Dave Emmons and anthro Col. (Ret.) Dr. Tom Sprague and their team recovered USAF Capt. David Joseph Phillips Jr. of Miami Beach, Florida. Flying with the 10th Fighter Commando Squadron out of Bien Hoa Air Base near Saigon, Captain Phillips's F-5C "Freedom Fighter" was shot down by automatic weapons fire on July 3, 1966. His remains were buried by locals, and JTF-FA conducted four investigations between 1993 and 2000 and the recovery operations in 2003 and 2004. Phillips's remains were identified by CIL in September 2004, and he was buried in July 2005 in Bonaventure Cemetery, Savannah, Georgia.

Out on the far Lao border in western Nghe An province, Capt. Joel Hendrickson, anthropologist Brad Sturm, and their team recovered USAF Lt. Col. Peter J. Frederick of Long Island City, New York. Flying from Takhli Royal Thai Air Force Base, Thailand, with the 355th Tactical Fighter Wing on a daylight armed reconnaissance mission on the Ho Chi Minh Trail near the Lao border, Lt. Col. Frederick was shot down in an F-105D "Thud" on March 15, 1967. His remains were identified by CIL in October 2006.

This joint field activity was the first time I had met Dr. Elizabeth Martinson Goodman, or "Zib," a young anthro fairly new to JPAC who seemed to have the favor of the gods. In Laos she was the one who found the remains of Charles Dean, brother of Governor Howard Dean, who at the time was campaigning for the presidency. I think she had found remains on every dig she had done thus far, including most of the crew of a crashed World War II cargo plane. When the anthros and I would get together for Tiger beer and platters of huge grilled prawns from one of huts on the beach at Da Nang, I would occasionally encourage their morale and determination by remarking that the rookie "Zib" had found more gold than all of them put together, with the exception, of course, of "Hoss" Moore.

Upon Dong Ma Mountain (elevation four thousand feet) in Quang Tri province, Capt. Grover Harms, anthro Dr. Elizabeth "Zib" Martinson Goodman, and their team recovered USMC Lt. Donald John Matocha, from Smithville, Texas, and the Texas A&M Class of 1967. Leading a patrol from Delta Company, 3rd Recon Battalion in a search for an observation post directing the shelling of Camp Carroll, Lieutenant Matocha was killed in a firefight on Dong Ma on April 5, 1968. Forced back down the mountain by enemy fire, marine patrols tried several times to return and recover the lieutenant's body, suffering another KIA in the process. An enemy squad leader, Nguyen Van Loc of the PAVN 320th Division buried Lieutenant Matocha near a bomb crater and contacted the detachment in 1996 as a witness. After several earlier recovery operations, Lieutenant Matocha's burial site was finally pinpointed by Dr. "Zib" Martinson Goodman.

Lieutenant Matocha was buried with full military honors on September 18, 2004, in Smithville, Texas. A thousand people attended the services, including fifty A&M classmates and a Marine Corps honor guard. He received a twenty-one-gun salute. Bagpipes wailed "Amazing Grace." Two buglers from the Aggie Band played echo taps.

Chapter 11

ÔNG, VĂN PHÒNG MIA–*HOA KỲ*

When I came to take command of the detachment and run the MIA recovery mission in Vietnam, I was determined to approach the duty with objective professionalism. I was the colonel and the *ông, Văn Phòng* MIA–*Hoa Kỳ,* boss or chief, Office of MIA–USA. Midway through the previous joint field activity my son Miles deployed to Iraq as a lieutenant in 3rd Brigade, 1st Infantry Division, the Big Red One. He crossed the Kuwait border in an unarmored Humvee for the three-day run to Baqubah, northeast of Baghdad. Suddenly my mission took on an entirely new meaning; it became a personal quest. I realized that in a flash I could join the fate of all those parents for whom we were trying to provide answers. I stopped watching the news on TV. As we closed out the last JFA I also realized that, because of this, I had become driven, intolerant of delay, impatient of inefficiency, and obsessive about preparations. In fact, Mr. Tu was probably not joking when he had said I had worn out everyone.

As soon as we finished writing our reports and the teams departed for Hawaii, we went straight into site reconnaissance for the seventy-seventh joint field activity, scheduled to start four weeks later, in April 2004.

Sergeant Revell, Buddy, and I drove through the morning mist to the Da Nang Airport to take a helicopter up the coast, then inland to check out a site a site west of Dong Ha. Glancing at the sky before boarding the aircraft, I knew anyone with any sense would have returned to the hotel to wait for another day. I looked at the pilots, who seemed casual about taking off in what was at best five-hundred meters' visibility and closing, meeting our flight minimums by a stretch. Strapping in, I was focused solely on my mission, which was to go to the site and ensure it was feasible for the next joint field activity. The pilots looked back at me, and I gave them a thumbs up without hesitation.

The aircraft rose, tilting toward the South China Sea to fly across Tourane Bay and up the coast. Halfway across the bay the fog closed in completely, and we were flying through soup. We had equipped the helicopters with weather radar and GPS, but I was not certain either was actually working or even turned on. The copilot had the weather radar screen turned toward him, so I was unable to observe it from my seat well behind them.

Once he was certain he was beyond the mountains at Hai Van Pass, the pilot dropped his speed to a crawl, slowly descending, crabbing toward the coast. Eventually we could distinguish the breakers and the sand strip of beach marking the coastline, two hundred feet below. For the next hour we crept up the coast, eyes straining for entrance to the Thach Han River, which we could track into Dong Ha. Following the middle of the river west, we scanned the fog ahead for power lines and other obstacles until at last we found the hilltop LZ, where we met the waiting vehicles.

After an hour's round trip and site visit, we were back aboard the helicopter, repeating in reverse our tortuous trip through the fog. As we finally neared Da Nang airport, I looked back in the cabin to study the faces of Philip Revell and Buddy Newell. They seemed very calm for such a harrowing flight. I realized then and there that, although I was willing to take a chance myself, I had carelessly and perhaps needlessly put them in jeopardy as well. They were both young. Buddy had a family to raise, and Philip was going to marry soon. The site visit could have waited for better weather, but my own hubris, stubbornness, and single-minded focus put us all at hazard, including the Vietnamese crew members, who were too proud and brave to signal that the *ông* had gone to stupid.

The Det mission had many inherent risks, but they were manageable. As commanders, we were trained to identify the risks and take mitigating measures to reduce them to a level we were willing to underwrite to accomplish a mission. There is a vast gulf between a risk and a gamble, and that day I gambled. On the ground I apologized to Philip and Buddy and vowed to myself it would never happen again.

Two weeks later, during the last of the joint advance work, we were driving down Route 1 in Quang Binh province when Buddy told Mr. Thinh to pull over. We got out of the vehicle, and Buddy pointed across the highway at a hill, the only one in the vicinity. Suddenly, without being told, I knew exactly why he had wanted to stop. That was the hill.

On April 7, 2001, nearly the entire Det 2 and nine accompanying Vietnamese officers were flying in the fog in an MI-17 that crashed into this hill. There were no survivors. It was believed they thought they were flying safely off the coast, but a strong wind had caused them to drift them inland. Killed that day were Lt. Col. Rennie M. Cory Jr., the detachment commander and an old friend of mine from our days at Fort Bliss; Lt. Col. George D. Martin, Rennie's replacement, who was in country doing his reconnaissance; USAF Maj. Charles E. Lewis, the Det XO; USAF M.Sgt. Steven L. Moser; TSgt. Robert M. Flynn; USN HMC Pedro J. Gonzales; and U.S. Army SFC Tommy J. Murphy. They all perished, along with the legendary Senior Colonel Tran Van Bien and eight other Vietnamese officers.

When I think about the tragedy, the first thing that comes to mind is the Vietnamese people who gave their lives trying to find answers for American families. We had a memorial plaque and monument on the front porch of the Det house. Every April 7 the Vietnamese bring flowers and burn joss sticks.

At the high-level technical talks in Hanoi and at the provincial coordination meeting in Da Nang, many of the officials complained that everyone was getting tired facing back-to-back joint field activities and that Chi Huy Truong (Lt. Col.) Smith pushed very hard, wearing them down on the seventy-sixth JFA with all that maneuvering from site to site. To which Lieutenant Colonel Smith replied that it was amazing how much we could all accomplish when we really put our minds to it. Nevertheless, I did get the message; they were right. I had some concern that back-to-back JFAs like we were doing, although necessary because of the weather window, did wear down both sides. Tired leaders make mistakes in judgment, and tired teams get careless and injured.

Fortunately, the pace and sites for the seventy-seventh JFA were fairly stable, with only one base camp. The remaining four teams could work from hotels or something nearly worthy of the name. The teams flew into Da Nang and appeared to be in good shape despite the fact that most of them had had only a few weeks' rest.

In Da Nang at that time we were using the Furama Beach Resort as a base of operations. The night before the teams showed up, a very large group of young Swedish tourists, some sort of corporate group symposium, arrived at the Furama. The next morning the group leader came to find me, saying they were planning a big beach party that night after their conference. However, she had heard that all these U.S. troops were going to arrive, so she wanted to meet with me to make sure my folks did not crash their company beach party.

As nicely as I could, I explained that I would tell the teams to stay away from her beach party, but these were very tough, red-blooded American military men and women who were coming to spend a month in the jungle. If her young people hooked up with my young people, there was nothing either of us could do about it, and it would help a lot if the young Swedish women would put on more clothes. As it turned out, apparently Swedish corporate people have no concept of a beach party. Our teams took one look at the goings-on and proclaimed it boring; most of them then went to downtown Da Nang to their favorite local spots.

After the operations order, the teams finished loading their trucks and headed to their sites, all of which were in central Vietnam, greatly simplifying the logistics and transportation requirements. All were fairly straightforward operations without the kind of major engineering efforts we had had to undertake in Vung Tau and Vinh. We had two "hotel-drive" sites in Quang Tri province, with the teams living in Dong Ha, and two "hotel-drive" sites in Quang Binh province, with the teams living in Dong Hoi. Only one team had a base camp on the Lao border in Thua Thien Hue province. All of this greatly reduced my worries about safety and health conditions, except, of course, the dangers of driving on the roads and the ever-present threat of malaria in central Vietnam.

Buddy and I flew back to Hanoi for two weeks before we started our next series of site visits to the teams. During this joint field activity, I probably did more public engagement than in any other period during my tour. Public engagement, or what I called "spreading the gospel," I considered a critical part of my duties as Det commander. The mission depended on political and public support, and we had developed a good, informative brief for politicians and the public.

To me it was more than just public relations, however, since I wanted to create informed audiences, as well as true believers. I lost count of the number of official visitors and congressional delegations I talked to, but I also kept my eye out for any opportunity to deliver the message. I briefed a group of American high school kids and their parents, who were in Hue on a summer education trip. Seeing they were the type that knew and talked to their congresspersons, I was more than happy to brief a group of well-to-do Californians on a bicycle tour of Vietnam. In Da Nang I gave the talk to a family from Austin just because the dad thought his three teenagers should know about the mission. When I first started, I had two versions; the first was businesslike and direct, while the second was what Buddy called the "leave 'em in tears" version.

One indelibly memorable talk occurred just before Buddy and I returned to Da Nang for site visits. The Det house welcomed Jan Scruggs and a delegation from the Vietnam Veterans Memorial Fund (VVMF), those who raised the money and oversaw the establishment of the wall in Washington, D.C. Jan, whom I had heard about for years, was the Vietnam vet who started the whole wall project. With them was Ann Sherman Wolcott, president of Gold Star Mothers, whose Ranger son was KIA in Vietnam. Most of the group of twenty were veterans on their first trip back, day number two; the energy level was off the scale.

The briefing went fine. The group seemed astonished at the level of effort put forth, the difficulty and the hazards presented by the operation, and the complete commitment to the mission by the government and our fine young men and women. We were all in tears before I was halfway finished. I ended by discussing my son Miles in Iraq and how his presence there brought me the perspective of a parent rather than that of just another commander on a mission. I added twenty extra prayers every night for his safe return.

At the end the group held a short memorial ceremony. Ann Wolcott made a little speech about this being her first trip to Vietnam and about how fortunate she suddenly felt because at least she had her son to put in Arlington National Cemetery. Her thoughts centered on all those mothers who did not but could live in hope we would find the answers. I was so drawn to her that I hugged and held her. We shed tears, holding hands for the rest of the visit. She said she would call Holly when she got back to say she had seen me and that I was doing fine. She made that call, and Holly was grateful.

Out of the group Andrew Carroll came up to have a long talk. I had seen him on *Booknotes.org.* He did the War Letters Home series for Scribner. He was doing a new book on letters from the home front and asked whether I could provide him a couple of letters I had written about the Det mission. Eventually I did, and he included them in *Behind the Lines: Powerful and Revealing American and Foreign Letters—and One Man's Search to Find Them* (New York: Scribner, 2005).

One day I had a request to brief the Australian defense attaché and a visiting Australian deputy minister on our MIA operations. Almost sixty thousand Australians served in Vietnam during the war, of whom five hundred were killed and three thousand wounded. Although they had no formal recovery program, they did have six military and two civilian MIA and were facing political pressure from private-interest groups such as Operation Aussies Home to make a deliberate search effort. With the help of Gary Flanagan I reviewed all we knew about Australian MIA cases before the meeting. I was not optimistic about their chances of success; they had three ground losses north of Bien Hoa, a helicopter crash with one solider last seen trapped under a burning helicopter somewhere north of Vung Tau, and a Canberra bomber with two crew members that simply vanished over Quang Nam province in the general vicinity of Da Nang. They had precious little information, no organization, and no formal contacts with the VNOSMP. Most of their questions at the briefing were focused on the practicalities, the complexities, and the expense of conducting operations in Vietnam.

Detachment 2 and JPAC were chartered strictly for efforts at recovering the U.S. missing; helping other nations was certainly outside our mission scope and politically sensitive as well. However, Australia had been a dear and faithful ally of the United States for almost a century, and I gave the defense attaché and the deputy minister all the information and encouragement I could. Frankly, I gave serious consideration to loaning them the investigative team to conduct a site survey or two but, after discussing it with Gary and Buddy, decided it was politically impractical. I was privately pessimistic they could ever launch a serious campaign. My pessimism, I am pleased to say, was proven wrong. From what I could follow in the press, a few years later the Australian government and private organizations began conducting a series of serious field operations, resulting in four recoveries in 2007. Detachment 2 offered advice, as well as expertise, but the Aussies were determined to conduct independent operations, which they did with success. The last of their military MIA, Flying Officer Michael Herbert and Pilot Officer

Robert Carver of the missing Canberra bomber, were announced recovered on July 30, 2009. Ironically, I was in Australia on the day of that announcement. As they say Down Under—Good on 'em.

Buddy and I returned south and, at the request of the JPAC Public Affairs Office, went to Hue to meet and brief a reporter doing a story on the mission. It turned out not to be a reporter but the author Caroline Alexander, who was writing an article for the *New Yorker.* Caroline had written one of my favorite books, *The Endurance: Shackleton's Legendary Antarctic Expedition.* We spent much of the time talking about writing and publishing history before she went off to spend some days with a couple of the teams. When the fog set in on the Lao border site and she could not fly out, she insisted she was up to walking out, spending most of a day in a tough jungle hump down the mountain with a team escort to the nearest road. There was nothing easy about this, and I was impressed when I found out. Had the team leader asked permission from me first, as he should have, I would have forbidden this risk. He and I had a little chat about that later, although Caroline told me afterward it was a great adventure.

Buddy and I spent a great deal of time that April and May 2004 sorting out an unusual number of oddball frustrations and complications that seemed to keep cropping up, so many in fact that we developed a new saying—"This is the most f***ed-up country I have ever seen; why do I love it so?"

On the Lao border the Van Kieu tribesmen of the local village decided they could not work for four days because the national elections were ten days

Back in the Khe Sanh: We are not lost, I think. *Courtesy Buddy Newell*

Quang Tri province. Buddy Newell: No problem, we go there.

Senior Col. Tau and I end a long day on the trail in Quang Nam province. *Courtesy Buddy Newell*

away and they needed to prepare. I dislike stereotypes, but the Van Kieu had a reputation for this sort of nonsense. I sent word to the tribal elders that I knew they could not read or write and had not the foggiest notion of what a national election was and that we were going to hire hard-working fishermen from the coast at Dong Ha and fly them in our helicopters up to the site to work. Well, I heard pretty quick from the provincial officials, who wanted to know why *Ông* Smith was trying to start a revolt among the Van Kieu. Fortunately, the Van Kieu soon came to their senses.

At another site the local landowner suddenly decided to demand three times the per-square-meter price we had agreed to when we negotiated the dig the month before. Also, he decided to add an outrageous parking fee of a dollar per vehicle for the team truck and van, two dollars a day for both vehicles. He concluded he had us over a barrel as the dig was well under way. After many conversations with Brigadier General "Que" Winfield in Hawaii, we decided we could not be held hostage because it would set a precedent that would spread.

Our Vietnamese VNOSMP counterparts understood the dilemma exactly and spent the day with province and village officials talking to the landowner, while I had the team at the hotel appearing to get ready to pack up and leave. Finally, one of our smart team sergeants came up with a brilliant idea to cut the Gordian knot.

We sent the team leader back to the landowner, apparently exhausted by all the officials and the captain formally refused to pay for added fees or parking. The team leader then asked the landowner whether he would please allow us to expand the site by seventy square meters at a dollar a square, to which he readily agreed. Of course, we had no use for the extra seventy square meters, nor did we ever touch the area. Seventy dollars saved a site, and everyone saved face.

The JFA became a struggle against the weather; terrific rain hampered the digs and crippled our ability to move around to sites by helicopter. Hue for the most part remained sunny and hot, while our sites in the provinces flooded. While waiting for the weather, I took the opportunity to see more of Hue, traveling around by bike-pedaled cyclo. I had thus far refused to ride in a cyclo, believing it to smack of colonial arrogance. However, one morning I walked all the way to the citadel, and my pulled hamstring prevented me from walking farther. As I looked around for a taxi, along came this very nice cycloman and handsome machine, freshly painted, with a shade roof to keep out the sun. I hopped in to go back to the hotel but found it fun, so I hired him to peddle me around Hue for an hour, much to the hard-working cycloman's appreciation for the income.

Buddy and I whiled away the afternoon drinking *soda chang duong* in the shade of our favorite sidewalk café on Hung Vuong Street. *Soda chang duong* (club soda, lime, sugar) is the ubiquitous Vietnamese hot-weather drink, made with a little lime juice and sliced lime in the bottom of a glass filled with club soda. Pour in a few spoons of sugar, and it bubbles up like a volcano.

Finally, by late evening the teams were beginning to report a break in the weather, so we continued our round of site visits the next morning, heading north to Dong Hoi.

Two weeks later, as the teams gathered in Da Nang for report writing and closeout before their return to Hawaii, my optimism brightened for the success of the effort. In spite of the difficulties with weather, we made two recoveries or, more precisely, definite progress toward final recoveries. Out in Quang Binh province on Kong Troi Mountain (Mountain without Clouds), near the Lao border, Capt. Octave "Mac" MacDonald and Dr. C. Elliott "Hoss" Moore and their team returned to a site opened the year before on the seventy-fourth JFA. This recovery operation and another on the next JFA brought home USAF Lt. Johnnie Clayton Cornelius from Williams AFB, Arizona, and Maj. Robert Francis Woods from Salt Lake City, Utah.

Flying out of Da Nang with the 20th Tactical Support Squadron, Lieutenant Cornelius and Major Woods were in their Cessna 02A "Skymaster" aircraft on June 26, 1968, flying a forward air controller mission just north of the DMZ, near the Lao border. After locating an NVA position, they rolled in low to mark it for the strike aircraft when the Cessna suddenly went into a sharp bank and crashed into the trees. Search and rescue flew overhead but did not locate a beeper, and ground search was impossible because of the enemy. The NVA buried the remains of the pilots, and JTF-FA conducted multiple surveys from 1993 to 1997 and four recovery operations from 2000 to 2004. Finally, in 2006 several witnesses helped locate the burial site. Major Woods was identified by CIL in February 2007, and Lieutenant Cornelius in May 2007. Lieutenant Cornelius was buried in November 2007 in Moore, Texas, and Major Woods was buried in Arlington National Cemetery in April 2008.

As we closed out the seventy-seventh JFA, the teams went back to Hawaii for no more than a month's rest before the third back-to-back joint field activity. Buddy and I went straight to the Da Nang Airport to start humping jungle for the recon of the next sites. We spent most of the week in the field before flying back to Hanoi.

Chapter 12
THE LAST FLIGHT

RETURNING TO HANOI, I had multiple messages and phone conversations with General Winfield over the ambassador's concerns about the upcoming repatriation ceremony, that it was becoming more about the USAF C-141 aircraft "Hanoi Taxi" than about the mission and sending home remains. The ambassador specifically inquired about the military decision-making process and the level at which the decisions about the ceremony were made.

The Hanoi Taxi was the aircraft that brought the original POWs home in 1973, their names autographed on the inside of the fuselage, and the air force was retiring it. There was this concept that had been approved by who knows who that it should be used on this repat for a last flight.

It did not help that the aircraft broke down en route, and we had to shift the whole ceremony a day, which did not endear us to the Vietnamese bureaucracy. The Vietnamese suddenly had an unusual interest in being precisely informed on exactly who was on the aircraft, what their role was, how we intended to conduct the ceremony, and so on. The media had considerable interest, and there was even a piece in the *London Times.*

We decided we would conduct the ceremony exactly as per standard operating procedure—no additions, no changes. I was confident everything would go fine for the ceremony, and since I was pretty lucky, the aging aircraft would probably get airborne again as well.

On the morning of May 28, 2004, the repatriation ceremony went just dandy. The aircraft took off again without a hitch, the prayers of everyone in the detachment and the embassy lifting it skyward. There were more press than usual, and they spent a good bit of time interviewing the pilot of the

Hanoi Taxi, a retiring U.S. Air Force Reserve major general who was a POW on the original flight.

In a wink we were back down in Da Nang receiving the team sergeants who were flying in to supervise the advance work on their sites, which had now become routine. A week later they were followed by the teams coming in from Hawaii.

Between joint advance work duties I spent my time carving a handle for my Vietnamese hand-forged axe, which I got because I did not have one. I began a collection of Vietnamese tools, knives, and machetes—not fancy stuff, mind you, but honest working tools. I bought my axe in the Dong Ha market for forty thousand *dong*, a good deal, not four dollars. For reasons unexplained, axes in Vietnam do not come with handles attached. Instead, they also hand you a tree limb from which to carve the handle. It is a special wood, extremely hard. When I asked the name of the wood, the market lady said it was called axe handle wood.

I set things up in my room in the Furama Resort to carve my axe handle with my Gerber multitool. The tree limb needed cutting, so I went and found the Furama maintenance supervisor, Mr. Hang, to see whether he could saw it for me. Having been an interpreter for the army back in the days of the war, Mr. Hang spoke excellent English. He had regained it after years in reeducation camps, then selling souvenirs to tourists up on Hai Van Pass. Four years previously an Australian engineer came along, the engineer who was building the Furama Resort. He needed an interpreter, so he hired Mr. Hang on the spot. Funny how life hangs on these random encounters. After Mr. Hang had spent three years translating instructions to the building crew on every aspect of the complex, the Furama management had enough sense to hire this very intelligent and lively fellow to be the chief of maintenance.

He offered to show me the carpenter shop where they made everything for the hotel. He had nine Lao carpenters, who stood passively while Mr. Hang explained every strange tool in the shop. I wanted to use a very interesting saw to cut my handle, but they would not allow it. Apparently it would be undignified, a loss of face for the Furama to let a guest do a little honest labor.

Returning to my suite, I pulled the glass top off the iron coffee table and rigged it up as a workbench. I transformed it into a vise with twenty feet of parachute cord twisted around the sawed-off half of the limb as a lever. Called a Chinese vise, I had learned about the tool in a wood shop in Hong Kong thirty years before, very handy in a pinch.

As a side note, in the West we anchor the piece we want to work on, putting the tool in our hand. In Asia they usually anchor the tool and work the piece in their hand, illustrating yet another gulf in our approach to life itself.

The domestic staff came in to clean the room and were very confused to see a tree limb tied to the coffee table, the floor covered in wood shavings, and me merrily whittling while singing along with Merle Haggard on the CD player. It was one of life's precious moments. They were very Vietnamese about it, pretending nothing at all was out of the ordinary, but as soon as possible they scurried out of the room, hiding laughter behind those tiny hands.

The axe and handle, soon very well joined, I left to soak in the sink for a day so the wood could swell to perfect union. The next morning the domestic staff found an axe in the sink, brightening up their day and giving them something to gossip about. I had Band-Aids on three cut fingers and blood on my best pair of shorts, but life was good.

In early June 2004 the teams came in good condition to start the seventy-eighth joint field activity, the third of back-to-back missions. After the operations order, they scattered to their sites, most of which were in central Vietnam. Considering the increasing wear and tear on the teams, I tried to keep everything as simple as possible.

Captain Grover Harms Jr. and anthro Dr. Pete Miller and their team had a most interesting site in Quang Nam province, southeast of Da Nang. The case was pure taphonomic science, a ground loss without burial, the result of a firefight in 1971. Thirty-seven-year-old Staff Sergeant Lewis C. Walton of Cranston, Rhode Island, served on a 5th Special Forces team of Task Force 1, Military Assistance Command Vietnam (MACV), Studies and Observation Group (SOG). On May 3, 1971, as part of Lam Son 719, the attack into Cambodia, Walton, two other Special Forces sergeants, and three indigenous tribesmen were inserted by helicopter near the Lao border. The team failed to make a planned radio contact the next day, and after a week of search-and-rescue flights they were declared MIA on May 10, 1971.

Eventually witnesses were found that indicated the vicinity of the fight and the fact that the NVA did not bury the American casualties. The recovery team's initial success on this JFA brought the teams back for the next for two years before CIL announced the recovery and identification of Sergeant First Class Lewis C. Walton in October of 2006. In May 2007 SFC Walton was buried in the Rhode Island Veterans Cemetery in Exeter, Rhode Island.

On June 21, 2004, I took my last flight in a Russian helicopter in Vietnam, going out to the Lao border to look at a site we were starting. Some were very superstitious about someone's last flight, and it was considered bad luck to fly with them because it would be testing the gods on that day. I wanted to leave Buddy behind, but he said he wasn't scared. I was. I had had some really attention-getting helo adventures, usually in fog or bad weather or trying to push a bird into a high mountain site against strong winds but was seldom concerned about it, having great faith in the skill of the Vietnamese senior colonel pilots who flew us. They were simply the best, still alive after two or more decades of flying helicopters around Vietnam. But the last flight, as everyone knew, was not about a pilot's skill; it was about luck, the mood of the gods, and your respect for them. Although I would have been happy to do the six-hour hike off the mountain and a five-hour SUV ride back to Da Nang, I forced myself onto the aircraft at the tiny, dust-covered landing zone at the site. We lifted off. The weather was perfect, almost no wind, sun shining, visibility endless, flight conditions as safe as could be. The ride back was the longest hour of that year in Vietnam. So, my last flight was done. As we touched down in Da Nang, I thought maybe it was time to go home.

I returned to Hanoi to pack out. I was happy but certainly melancholy about leaving Vietnam. That night the detachment and Vietnamese staff and workers had a going-away party. I told them I came to Vietnam three decades ago as a boy and left as a man and that that experience had been a major influence in my life. This time, to come back, I had to once again leave my family and my country, but I found a new country and a new family. The staff and house girls were my sisters and daughters, and my brothers were our drivers, who carried me safely over thousands of miles of dangerous roads. I was sad to leave this new family. The house girls flattered me by bawling like babies, tears all around, but this came as no surprise because the Vietnamese are so emotional, wearing their hearts right on their sleeve. After a while, when the *cuoc lui* and beer got to flowing freely, my Oklahoma cowboy, U.S. Marine deputy Major Tom Dicken and I conducted an exercise in trying to teach them to dance the Texas two-step and Cotton-eyed Joe. Hilarious would be the proper description of the outcome.

It had been an extraordinary year, full of exotic adventure, personally fulfilling, carrying out a most rewarding duty to the MIA families. In the end I had the honor to be a part of finding fourteen lost ones to send back home. It was the best assignment in my three decades of service. I was proud to command the remarkably dedicated young military men and women who spend months in the harsh jungle without a grumble or single word of complaint to accomplish the mission. They made me completely humble to serve beside them. It was an honor to share their company and friendship. It also made me proud to be an American. We have an iron-clad commitment to our military and their families. If they are lost, we will do whatever it takes to find them. As a professional soldier and the father of a son who was serving in Iraq, I found this commitment by the American people extraordinary. No other nation on earth makes it, means it, and keeps it. I was just grateful to have played a small part in keeping that promise.

At the last technical talks my Vietnamese government counterparts made a little official farewell note of regret at my pending departure, a perfectly normal diplomatic acknowledgement, routine—except when Mr. Pham Van Que used the words *xuất sắc* to describe their respect for our relationship. I noticed the American Vietnamese speakers on our side rock back a bit in their chairs and exchange glances. Buddy took a long, flustered pause before he translated. They told me later the term is nearly impossible to translate and is a special form of reserved honor. In all their many years here they had never before heard it applied to an American. So, I guess I must have done okay. It wasn't hard really, simple, just a matter of making sure we focused on our shared mutual interest and never ever forcing them to lose face. The fact is I had a deep respect for the Vietnamese. We could learn much from them, and they have much to learn from us. Such is our future together, and I wanted to be a part of it.

After the change of command with Special Forces Lt. Col. Lenfort "Mitch" Mitchell, Mr. Thinh drove me to the airport for the last flight home. Sixteen hours of flying gave me plenty of time to reflect on what I had learned. In all our chum-for-chum drinking sessions and all of the very difficult and dangerous spots we had shared, I had learned something from them. The Vietnamese taught me that life is not linear at all; it loops back and back, circles within circles. But then again, these are the same people that speed on a motorbike, dad driving, small son between his knees, wife balanced on the back clutching a baby in one arm and a basket of fruit in the other. I went there this time as a raja of the imperial court but came away a very humbled student of life and the human heart. My mentors were slant eyed, wise, and wiry: peasant farmers, cyclomen, street vendors, house girls, my drivers, expats, the occasional drunken writers, poets, and artists. We are all each and every one but simple travelers in the dark wilderness, seeking light on the far horizon. Matters of the heart are so sublime, yet so savage. We in our Western world tend to seek only those moments of happiness and joy and avoid those searing pains of the heart. But the Vietnamese seem to equally embrace joy and sadness with the same intensity, keeping the heart in balance. They take the laughter of life with full measure but equally cherish the heartache. It is the pain that creates their art and soul. Maybe that is why Vietnam is so extraordinary.

Afterword
NOVEMBER 2009

WILLIAM "BUDDY" NEWELL still continues the MIA mission at Hanoi Detachment 2, nearly two decades after he was the first to arrive in 1992.

My son Miles Smith returned safely from Iraq and is a U.S. Army Reserve captain. He lives in Perth, Australia, where he works as an exploration geologist in the Australian outback.

After returning from Vietnam in 2004, I had a number of follow-on assignments: head, Military History Department, U.S. Army Command and General Staff College; director, Combat Studies Institute, Fort Leavenworth, Kansas; garrison commander, Fort Riley, Kansas; and deputy director, West Region, Installation Management Command. After military retirement as a colonel in October 2009 I continued government service as a proud Department of the Army civilian at Fort Sam Houston, Texas.

INDEX

A-1A Skyraider aircraft, 63, 90
A-6A Intruder aircraft, 90
acupuncture, oriental medicine, 101–103
A Shau Valley, Vietnam, 11, 12
Alexander, Caroline, 117
Amari Hotel, Bangkok, Thailand, 96
An Khe, Vietnam, 53
Arizona Memorial, U.S.S., 96
Arlington National Cemetery, 22, 28, 69, 86, 90, 115, 120
artemesia (herb), 102
Australia: 44, 73, 76; Australian MIAs in Vietnam, 116–17; Operation Aussies Home, 116
avian flu (H5N1 Virus), 104–105

Baghdad, Iraq, 111
Ball, Allaine, 14, 41, 93
Ball, Col. Steve, 14, 41, 93
Bangkok, Thailand, 3, 8, 76, 96
Baqubah, Iraq, 111
Bassac River, Cambodia, 78
Ba Trieu St., Hanoi, Vietnam, 38
Beijing, China, 10, 76
Bellard, Scott, 31
Benedix, Derek, 84–86
Bergen-Belsen Concentration Camp, Germany, 77
Berlin, Germany, 10
Bien Hoa, Vietnam, 109, 116
Bien, Senior Col. Tran Van, 113
Bloomfield, Mo., 22
Bonaventure Cemetery, Savannah, Ga., 109
Bright Light (data base), 58
Buckingham, Lt. Col. Dave, 52
Buon Ma Thuot, Vietnam, 50
Burghardt, Ambassador Raymond F., 13, 14, 121
Burma, 79

C-17 Globemaster aircraft, 23, 25, 30, 71, 72
C-123 Provider aircraft, 22
C-141 Starlifter "Hanoi Taxi" aircraft, 121–22
Cambodia, Royal Kingdom of: 3, 50, 51, 76–79, 123; Pol Pot terror, 77
Camp Carroll, Vietnam, 110
Camp Smith, Hi., 6
Camus, Albert, 68
Canada, 51
Caravelle Hotel, Ho Chi Minh City, Vietnam, 10, 25
Carlisle Barracks, Pa., 1, 2, 6
Carmina Burana (opera), 45
Carroll, Andrew, 115–16

Carter, Maj. James L., 22
Carver, Pilot Officer Robert, 117
Cat Cat, Vietnam, 100
Cathay Pacific Airlines, 8
Central Identification Laboratory (CIL), 3, 5, 22, 28, 69, 71, 80, 81, 90, 96, 109, 120, 124
Cessna O-2A Skymaster aircraft, 120
China, 3, 39
China Beach, Da Nang, Vietnam, 16, 23, 24
Citadel, Hue, Vietnam, 71, 72
Cornelius, Lt. Johnnie Clayton, 120
Cory, Lt. Col. Rennie M., Jr., 2, 113
Cory, Thomas, 71, 72
Cranston, R.I., 123
Cuba, 10, 31
cuoc lui (moonshine), 88, 124

Da Mon Toi, Vietnam, 90
Da Nang, Vietnam, 5, 11, 13, 14, 16, 21, 22, 30, 32, 50, 61, 105, 108, 109, 111–14, 120, 122
Dac Lac Province, Vietnam, 50
Dac Nong Province, Vietnam, 50
Dai Nam flag, Vietnam, 32
Dak To (city), Vietnam, 50
Dalat, Vietnam, 26, 104
Dallas, Tex., 26
Dao, Nguyen Van, 31–32, 52, 53–54
Dean, Charles, 109
Dean, Gov. Howard, 109
Defense Language School, 60
Defense POW/Missing Personel Office (DPMO), 3
Demilitarized Zone (DMZ), 63, 81, 120
Dicken, Maj. Tom, 30, 44–46, 87, 101, 124
doi moi (new economy), 52
Dong Ha, Vietnam, 22, 62, 63, 69, 111, 112, 114, 118
Dong Hoi, Vietnam, 81, 114, 120
Dong Ma Mountain, Vietnam, 109–110
Duong Dien Bien Phu St., Hanoi, Vietnam, 31

East Berlin, Germany, 96
El Paso, Tex., 30
Emmons, Capt. Dave, 89, 109
Empress Hotel, Dalat, Vietnam, 104

F-4 Phantom aircraft, 20
F-5C Freedom Fighter aircraft, 109
F-105 Thunderchief "Thud" aircraft, 84, 86, 109
Fall, Bernard, 24
Father Charlie (priest), 41
Fayetteville, N.C., 69
Fighter Attack Squadron 52 (VA-52) USN, 90
1st Air Commando Squadron, USAF, 90
1st Infantry Division (Big Red One), 2, 6, 111
5th Special Forces, 123
Flanagan, Keith Gary, 30, 32–34, 51, 53, 62, 65, 66, 116
Florence, Italy, 10
Flores, Chief Warrant Officer, 17
Flynn, Tech. Sgt. Robert M., 113
Fort Benning, Ga., 2, 81
Fort Bliss, Tex., 2, 113
469th Tactical Fighter Squadron, USAF, 86
France, 51, 101
Frederick, Lt. Col. Peter J., 109
French Foreign Legion, 81
Furama Resort, Da Nang, Vietnam, 16, 23, 113, 114, 122

Galindo, Sgt. Urbano, 30
Garden Grove, Cal., 32
George, Kysa, 40
George, Lt. Col. Jay, 6–7, 40
Germany, 2

Gia Lai Province, Vietnam, 50, 53, 58
Giang, Pham Trong, 53
Gold Star Mothers, 115
Gonzales, Hospital Corpsman Pedro J., 113
Goodman, August, 62
Griffiths, Ann Mills "A.M.G.," 2–3
Group 559, PAVN, 31

Hale Koa Military Hotel, Hi., 95
Ha Long Bay, Vietnam, 82, 90, 100–101
Ha Long City, Vietnam, 82
Ha Tinh City, Vietnam, 84
Ha Tinh Province, Vietnam, 84
Hai Ba Trung Street, Hanoi, Vietnam, 95, 98
Hai Van Pass, Vietnam, 24, 112
Hamburger Hill (Apbia Mnt.), 11
Hamilton, Col. Eugene D., 86
Hanauma Bay Nature Preserve, Hi., 96
Hang Dau St., Hanoi, Vietnam, 15
Hang Gai Street, Hanoi, Vietnam, 35, 95
Hang, Mr., 122
Hanna, Sgt. 1st Cl. Kenneth, 58–59, 69, 80
Hanoi Hilton Prison. See Hoa Lo Prison.
Hanoi Opera House, Hanoi, Vietnam, 32, 45
Hanoi, Vietnam, 2, 3, 9, 20, 24, 29, 76, 82, 84, 95; description, 10, 25, 35–46, 96–97
Harms, Capt. Grover, Jr., 109, 123
Hawaii, 4, 5, 23, 50, 95–96
Hawes, Col. Sam, 28
Hawley, Lt. Col. Steve, 2, 7, 8, 10, 26
helicopters: ; CH-47 Chinook, 26; MI-8, 10, 26; MI-17, 11, 12, 82, 88, 113; flight operations, 59–60, 111–12, 113, 119
Hendrickson, Capt. Joel, 109
Herbert, Flying Officer Michael, 116
Hickam Air Force Base, Hi., 3, 4
Hien, Mr., People's Committee Deputy Chairman, 64
Hilton Opera Hotel, Hanoi, Vietnam, 37, 44
Hites, Dickie, 52
H'mong. *See* Vietnam, minority tribes
Ho Chi Minh City (HCMC), Vietnam, 10, 24, 25, 35, 79, 105
Ho Chi Minh Trail, Vietnam,20, 31, 109
Hoa Lo Prison (Hanoi Hilton), 35
Hoa, Mrs. (Admin Asst.), 42, 43, 73
Hoan Kiem Lake, Hanoi, Vietnam, 35, 95
Hong Kong, China, 123
Honolulu, Hi., 6, 7, 95
Hue, Vietnam: 11, 30, 61, 62, 63, 69; description, 69–71, 117, 119
Hung Vuong St., Hue, Vietnam, 119
Huong, Dr. Tran Thanh, 101–103
Huong Hoa District, Vietnam, 65

Indonesia, 25
Iraq, 2, 6, 111, 115, 125, 127

Jaje, Dora, 76
Jaje, Lt. Col. Mike, 76
Joint Casualty Resolution Center (JCRC), 3
Joint POW/MIA Accounting Command (JPAC), 3, 80, 96
Joint Task Force-Full Accounting (JTF-FA), 3, 4, 6, 41, 60
Joint Task Force-Full Accounting (JTF-FA) and Joint POW/MIA Accounting Command (JPAC): Detachment 1, Bangkok, 3, 8, 76, 77, 93; Detachment 2, Hanoi, 3, 4, 14, 41, 42, 60, 113, 116; Detachment 3, Vientiane, 3, 73, 74; Investigative Team (IT), 4, 19, 26, 31, 51, 53, 58, 59, 81, 90, 116; Joint Advance Work, 93, 111–112; Joint

Joint Task Force-Full Accounting (JTF-FA) and Joint POW/MIA Accounting Command (JPAC) (*continued*)
Field Activity (JFA), 4, 22,47, 80, 93, 104, 108–109, 111,113, 119, 123; Joint Forensic Review (JFR), 5; logistics,49–50, 82, 96; operations, 4–5, 7, 10–11, 14, 16, 19–21, 26–27, 30–34, 46–50, 56–57, 63–69, 71, 82, 84–86, 87–89, 90–92, 93, 108–110, 111–12, 113, 116, 119, 120,123–24; provincial coordination meetings, 47–48, 57–59, 104, 113; Recovery Team (RT), 4,18; Research and Investigative Team (RIT), 4, 31, 54; repatriation ceremony, 71–72, 104, 121; technical talks, 47–48, 52, 58, 113
Joint Task Force-Six (JTF-6), Fort Bliss Tex., 2

Kansas,17
Kent, Capt. Geoff, 26, 27, 28
Key West, Fla., 97
Khai, Vietnamese Prime Minister Phan Van, 58
Khe Sanh Siege, 62–63
Khe Sanh, Vietnam, 22, 62, 63, 64, 117
Khmer Rouge, 77
Khmer tribe, Cambodia, 76, 77
Khoi, Senior Colonel, Pham Cong, 87–89
Kien Giang Province, 108–109
Kitty Hawk, US Navy Aircraft Carrier, 90
Kon Tum (city), Vietnam, 50
Kon Tum Province, Vietnam, 50
Kong Troi Mountain, Vietnam, 120
Korat Royal Thai Air Force Base, Thailand, 86
Korea: 41; Korean MIA in Vietnam, 41
Korean War, 3
Kuwait, 111
Kyrgyzstan, 1

Lam Son 719, 123
Lan Xang Ave., Vientiane, Laos, 75
Lang Vei Special Forces Camp, Vietnam, 58, 62–63, 90
Lang Vei, Vietnam, 62, 63, Lanham, Capt. Eric, 91
Lao Airlines, 90
Lao Bao beer, 79
Lao Cai, Vietnam, 97, 98, 99
Laos, 3, 11, 50, 65, 66, 68, 73–76
Lapham, Maj. Robert G., 90
La Porte, Ind., 69
Laredo, Tex., 76
Le Thai To St., Hanoi, Vietnam, 95
Le Tru Tich (Tet ritual), 101
Lewis, Maj. Charles E., 113
Light Attack Squadron Four (VAL-4) "Black Ponies" USN, 26
Lindewald, M.Sgt. Charles Wesley, Jr., 63, 69, 80
Loc, Nguyen Van, 110
London, England, 10
London Times, 121
Long Island City, N.Y., 109
Long, Capt. Carl Edwin, 26–28, 80
Long Tau shipping channel, Vietnam, 26
Los Angeles, Cal., 25

Macdonald, Capt. Octave "Mac," 120
Man, Mr., Local Party Secretary, 63
Manhasset, N.Y., 90
Manila, Philippines, 10
Mao, Senior Colonel, 63
Marble Mountain (Ngu Hanh Son), Da Nang, Vietnam, 16, 17
Marshall, Mich., 90
Martin, Lt. Col. George D. "Marty," 2, 113

Martinson Goodman, Dr. Elizabeth "Zib," 109–110
Matocha, Lt. Donald John, 109–110
Mekong Delta, Vietnam, 10, 16, 23, 25
Mekong River, 74, 78, 79
Metro Store, Hanoi, Vietnam, 40
Mexico, 96
Miami Beach, Fl., 109
Mig aircraft, 16, 23
Military Assistance Command Vietnam (MACV), 123
Miller, Dr. Pete, 11, 26, 30, 32–34, 62, 65, 68, 91, 123
Missouri Veterans Cemetery, 22
Mitchell, Lt. Col. Colonel Lenfort "Mitch," 125
Mobile, Ala., 60
Moc Chau, Vietnam, 88, 89
Monkey Mountain, Da Nang, Vietnam, 24
Moore, Dr. C. Elliot "Hoss" II, 17–18, 22, 90, 109, 120
Moore, Tex., 120
Moser, M.Sgt. Steven L., 113
Mossman, Lt. Harry S., 90
moxa leaf, 102
moxibustion, 102
Murphy, Sgt. 1st Cl. Tommy J., 113
Museum of Ethnology, Hanoi, Vietnam, 46
My, Miss (chief laundress), 42, 43, 108

Nam Dinh Province, Vietnam, 55
Nam, Hoang, 58, 59, 67, 69
Narita Airport, Tokyo, Japan, 7, 96
National League of Families, 3
Naugatuck, W.V., 22
Newell, Diep, 60
Newell, Megan, 60
Newell, William H. "Buddy," III, 10, 12, 16, 17, 22, 25, 26, 27, 30, 45, 48, 53, 58, 59, 60–61, 62, 64–66, 70, 80, 81, 84–89, 93, 101, 104, 105–107, 111–12, 113, 115, 116, 117, 118, 127
The New Yorker, 117
New Zealand, 73
Nghe An Province, Vietnam, 55, 109, 110
Ngu Hanh Son, Vietnam. *See* Marble Mountain
Ninh Binh Province, Vietnam, 55
Noi Bai Airport, Hanoi, Vietnam, 5, 8, 16, 71, 72, 104
North Vietnamese Army (NVA). *See* Peoples Army of North Vietnam (PAVN)

Okinawa, Japan, 60
Oklahoma, 44
Orner, Lt. Col. Tim, 6, 83, 96
OV-10 Bronco aircraft, 26, 27

Paris, France, 75
Parks, Master Sergeant Mike, 50
Parsley, Sgt. Edward M., 22
Pasadena, Cal., 22
Patterson, Joel, 52
Patuxai Victory Gate, Vientiane, Laos, 75–76
Peoples Army of North Vietnam (PAVN), 31, 62, 63, 90, 120
Pepperall, Ala., 86
Peppers, Lt. Col. Mike, 2
Perfume River, Hue, Vietnam, 70
Perth, Australia, 127
Phang Kham Road, Vientiane, Laos, 75
Philippines, 75
Phillips, Capt. David Joseph, Jr., 109
Phnom Penh, Cambodia: 77; description, 77–79
Phu Bai Airport, Hue, Vietnam, 81
Pleiku, Vietnam, 50, 54, 58, 90
Pol Pot, 77
Porter, Ray, 10
Prague, Czech Republic, 10

Preah Ang Phanauvong St., Phnom Penh, Cambodia, 78

Quang Binh Province, Vietnam, 2, 81, 82, 112, 114, 120
Quang Nam Province, Vietnam, 49, 105, 116, 118, 123
Quang Ninh Province, Vietnam, 82, 83, 100
Quang Tri Province, Vietnam, 22, 58, 62, 63, 64, 67, 90, 114, 118
Que, Pham Van, 125

Ray, M.Sgt. Kelly, 31
Redmann, Brig. Gen. Steven J., 7, 13, 14, 15, 52, 54
Redmann, Kate, 14
Redmann, Pat, 14
Revell, Sgt. Philip, 43, 50, 105, 107, 111–112
Rhode Island Veterans Cemetery, Exeter R.I., 124
Rio Grande River, 49
Rome, Italy, 101
Route 1, Vietnam, 24–25, 55, 56, 63, 93, 112
Route 6, Vietnam, 84
Route 9, Vietnam, 63, 65, 66
Royale Hotel, Vung Tau, Vietnam, 25

S-21 Prison Camp, Cambodia. *See* Toul Sleng High School
Saigon Morin Hotel, Hue, Vietnam, 69
Saigon River, Vietnam, 25, 28, 30
Saigon, Vietnam. *See* Ho Chi Minh City
Salt Lake City, Ut., 120
San Antonio, Tex., 16
Sandberg, USN Lt.(jg) Joel A., 26
San Francisco, Cal., 81
Sa Pa, Vietnam, 13, 97–100
Scranton, S. C., 69
Scruggs, Jan. C., 115
Seventh Fleet, U.S. Navy, 16
Shackelton's Antarctic Expedition, 117
Sisowath Quay, Phnom Penh, Cambodia, 78
Smith, Dustin, 2, 95, 98, 99–101
Smith, Holly, 2, 30, 95–101, 115
Smith, Miles T., 2, 6, 111, 115, 127
Smithville, Tex., 109, 110
Son La Province, Vietnam, 84, 87, 89
Song Da River, 84, 87
South China Sea, 4, 25, 55, 79, 82, 112
Spain, 102
Spanish influenza of 1918, 105
Sprague, Col. (Ret.) Dr. Tom, 109
Strain, Lt. Col. Johnny, 73
Street Without Joy (*La rue sans joie*), 24
Studies and Observation Group, (SOG), 123
Sturm, Brad, 109
Styx, River (Greek mythology), 62
Suvarnabhumi Airport, Bangkok, Thailand, 8, 96
Sydney, Australia, 10

10th Fighter Commando Squadron, USAF, 109
311th Cargo Squadron, USAF, 22
355th Tactical fighter Wing, USAF, 109
320th Division, PAVN, 110
20th Tactical Support Squadron, USAF, 120
Takhli Royal Thai Air Force Base, Thailand, 109
Ta Phin, Vietnam, 98, 99
Tahoma National Cemetery, 90
Tajikistan, 1
Talat Sao (Morning Market), Vientiane, Laos, 76
Tam Dao Mountain (Thud Ridge), Vietnam, 8
Tam, Ms., (cook), 15, 40, 104
Tan Hao Hamlet, Vietnam, 65
Tan Lien Village, Vietnam, 65

Tan Son Nhat Airport, Ho Chi Minh City, Vietnam, 25
taphonomic science, 18
Tau, Senior Colonel, 118
Tay Ho Lake, Hanoi, Vietnam, 10, 14, 34, 36, 43
Taylor, Lt. Col. John "J. T.," 2, 7
Tet (Vietnamese New Year), 95, 101
Tet 1968 (battle), 25, 62, 70
Texas A&M University, 1, 2, 26, 28, 109, 110
Texas State University, 2
Thach Han River, Vietnam, 112
Thai Hoa Palace, Hue, Vietnam, 70
Thailand, 3, 13, 23, 96
Than Hoa Province, Vietnam, 55
thien huony (herb), 102
Thinh, Dang Van (driver), 8–9, 15, 17, 22, 57, 69, 84, 96, 112
Thua Thien-Hue Province, Vietnam, 11, 13, 25, 114
Thud Ridge. *See* Tam Dao Mountain, Vietnam
tiger balm, 82
Tiger beer, 34, 109
Tiger Tooth Mountain, Vietnam, 63, 64
Titus Andronicus, William Shakespeare, 62
Tonle Sap River, Cambodia, 78
Toul Sleng High School (S-21 Prison), Phnom Penh, Cambodia, 77
Tourane Bay, Da Nang, Vietnam, 112
Tran Quoc Pagoda, Hanoi, Vietnam, 36, 37
Truong Sanh Palace, Hue, Vietnam, 70
Truong Tien Bridge, Hue, Vietnam, 70
Tu, Tran Van, 14, 31, 57, 59, 62, 63, 67, 69, 72, 84, 86, 91, 108, 111
Tuan, Mr. (police chief), 64

U.S. Air Force, 30, 34, 93
U.S. Ambassador, Vietnam. *See* Burquart, Raymond
U.S. Army Special Forces, 62–63, 69
U.S. Army War College, Carlisle Barracks, Pa., 1, 101
U.S. Embassy, Bangkok, Thailand, 93
U.S. Embassy, Hanoi, Vietnam, 3, 4, 13, 51, 93
U.S. Embassy, Vientiane, Laos, 76
U.S. House of Representatives, 53
U.S. Marine Corps, 28, 71, 87, 110
U.S. MIA Office (*Văn Phòng* MIA-*Hoa Kỳ*), Hanoi, Vietnam, 4, 39, 47, 86, 111
United Nations, 31, 49, 101
U.S. Navy, 1
United States Department of Defense, 3
United States Department of State, 3, 51
United States Military Academy, West Point, N.Y, 1, 2, 19
United States Pacific Command, 7
Uzbekistan, 1

Victoria Hotel, Sa Pa, Vietnam, 96
Vientiane, Laos, 3, 73–76, 78
Viet Cong, 17, 25, 62
Viet Minh Revolution, 55
Vietnam Airlines, 10, 16, 37, 73, 76, 77, 96
Vietnam: 1, 3, 4, 77, 115, 123, 126; Buddhists, 56; disease, 10, 104–105, 114; economy, 52; internet, 52; jungle, 11, 82; people, 15, 28, 37–40, 43, 45–46, 55, 74, 76, 80, 82, 85–86, 99–100, 101, 105–107, 119, 122–23, 125, 126; roads, 15, 16, 25, 37, 38, 55, 69, 77, 84, 100, 114; terrain, 25, 100, 106, 107; weather, 43–44, 80, 119
Vietnam, minority tribes: 46; Black H'mong, 98; Black Thai, 46; Bru, 62; Ca, 62; Chu-ru, 63; Co-tu, 105–107; Dao, 99; Giay, 99; H'mong, 46, 51, 63, 99; Mon-Khmer, 46;

Vietnam, minority tribes (*continued*)
"Montagnards," 46; Red Dao, 46, 83, 98, 99; Tay, 100; Van Kieu, 117–118
Vietnam, Socialist Republic of, government: 4, 8, 15, 32, 93; Army, *See* Peoples Army of Vietnam (PAVN); Communist Party, 37; military-to-military relations with U.S., 57, 93; Ministry of Foreign Affairs, Americas Department, 15; Ministry of Public Security, 15; Vietnamese Office for Seeking Missing Persons (VNOSMP), 15, 30, 31, 32, 47, 49, 84, 86, 116, 119
Vietnam Human Rights Amendment, U.S. State Department authorization bill, 31–32, 53
Vietnam Veterans Memorial Fund, 115
Vietnam Veterans of America, 71, 72
Vietnam War (American War), 3, 55
Vinh, Vietnam, 48, 56–57, 58, 84, 86, 90–92
Virginia, 14
Vung Tau, Vietnam, 10, 11, 23, 25–26, 27, 28, 58, 80, 116

Waikiki Beach, Honolulu, Hi., 6, 95
Waller, Sgt. Therman M., 22
Walter Reed Hospital, 102
Walton, Sgt. 1st Cl. Lewis C., 123–24
War Remembrance Museum (American War Crimes Museum), Ho Chi Minh City, Vietnam, 25
Ward, Ron, 31, 54
Washington, D.C., 2, 7, 31, 73, 74, 115
Williams Air Force Base, Az., 120
Winfield, Brig. Gen. W. Montague "Que," 80, 95–96, 119, 121
Wolcott, Ann Sherman, 115
Wolfgram, Capt. Ryan, 90
Woods, Maj. Robert Francis, 120
World Trade Organization (WTO), 25
World War II, 3
Wynne, Ark., 22

Xuan Dieu Street, Hanoi, Vietnam, 38, 41
Xuan Huong Lake, Dalat, Vietnam, 104

Young, Daniel, 25, 30, 49–50

Zukowsky, Capt. Shawn, 22